Collins Big Cat

Assessment and Support Guide A

Series editor: Cliff Moon

William Collins' dream of knowledge for all began with the publication of his first book in 1819. A self-educated mill worker, he not only enriched millions of lives, but also founded a flourishing publishing house. Today, staying true to this spirit, Collins books are packed with inspiration, innovation and practical expertise. They place you at the centre of a world of possibility and give you exactly what you need to explore it.

Published by Collins
An imprint of HarperCollins*Publishers*
77–85 Fulham Palace Road
Hammersmith
London
W6 8JB

Browse the complete Collins catalogue at
www.collinseducation.com

10 9 8 7 6 5 4 3 2 1

ISBN 978-0-00-726572-5

British Library Cataloguing in Publication Data
A Catalogue record for this publication is available from the British Library

Credits
Book by book notes and PCM writers: Karina Law and Niki Foreman
Guided reading and assessment notes writers: Maoliosa Kelly and Helen Mundy
Guided reading and assessment consultant: Laura Ellen Sharp
Series editor: Cliff Moon
Design managers: Nicola O'Reilly and Nicola Kenwood
Designer: Neil Adams
Illustrations: Maggie Brand, Steph Dix, Bridget Dowty and Sarah Wimperis
Photography: Steve Lumb

Printed and bound by Martins the Printers, Berwick Upon Tweed

You might also like to visit
www.harpercollins.co.uk
The book lover's website

This book is proudly printed on paper which contains wood from well-managed forests, certified in accordance with the rules of the Forest Stewardship Council. For more information about FSC, please visit www.fsc.org

Mixed Sources
Product group from well-managed
forests and other controlled sources
www.fsc.org Cert no. SW-COC-1806
© 1996 Forest Stewardship Council
FSC

Contents

A Letter from Cliff Moon

Series editor, *Collins Big Cat*

Dear Colleague

I'd like to start with a parable, paraphrased from Robert O'Brien's 1971 children's novel, *Mrs Frisby and the Rats of NIMH* (Puffin Modern Classics):

> *Once upon a time a group of laboratory rats learnt to read. First they were taught letters and their associated sounds but that didn't mean a great deal because, as the rats said, "we didn't know what reading was" and "as to what all this was for, none of us had any inkling"*

> *But then one day the penny dropped. The rats saw a sign which said 'R-A-T-S', remembered the picture which went with the word, and realised what reading was: ... "using symbols to suggest a picture or an idea." Eventually they were able to read the instructions for opening their cages and that led to their escape ...*

> **"By teaching us to read, [the scientists] had taught us how to get away."**

Now there's a purpose for teaching reading. Everything we do about reading should help children to *get away*; away into a world of fantasy, away into information gathering, and away into seeing the world through others' eyes. If we only have a single aim in teaching reading then it should be to get children to want to read under the bedclothes with a torch (figuratively speaking). That implies their having access to reading material which is worth the effort and books they can't put down.

How do we learn?

There is little evidence to suggest that we learn different things in different ways. Take riding a bike, for instance. When you learn to ride a bike you don't do discrete exercises in ankle movements, leg pushing, handlebar gripping, balancing; subsequently joining two, three, four exercises. That would be the easiest way to fall off! No, when a child has a bike for the first time, what do we see? Adults running alongside, holding the saddle, supporting the child no matter how much wobbling occurs in the process. The child is using ankles, legs, arms and hands to ride the bike shakily until

balance, control and confidence are achieved. That's how we all learn new skills: by getting every strategy working in unison from the beginning and refining the details later.

Consider how children learn to talk. On average their increase in two-word utterances ranges from one or two at 18 months to 2,500 at 24 months. Two-word utterances like *mummy car* and *daddy work* say everything they need to express.

Think about the feedback that children receive from their carers who pick up on what children *mean* and not the form in which it's said.

Learning to read

This brings us to reading. Is learning to read somehow different from learning other skills? It is just as holistic an activity as anything else. In order to read fluently you have to co-ordinate a whole range of strategies at the same time. Just like the child careering on the bike or using two-word utterances, you have to get every strategy working in unison from the start. That means having lots of material to practise on at a very basic level.

Children should be seen as readers from the moment they open their first book, or notice an item of junk mail, or see their first advert on television. There is a huge body of evidence which supports the very early development of emergent literacy. Children hypothesise about print as soon as their eyes can focus. So learning to read is a holistic skill too and children entering school, whatever their background experience, have already learnt a great deal about reading and print.

Learning to love reading

Some years ago, a researcher, interviewing children about their reading, asked a seven-year-old boy why he was learning to read at school. "So I can stop," he replied. What this illustrates is that unless we promote positive attitudes to reading at every stage of the learning-to-read process, then we are wasting our time. No one has summed this up better than Margaret Meek (alias Spencer), an eminent commentator on children's books and reading, when she said:

> *The way children are taught to read tells them what adults think literacy is.*

So spend a little time examining what you think literacy is and translate that into your teaching. Does it help you *get away*, enrich your experience, give you pleasure, make you laugh, cry, hope?

Literature in literacy

Two other statements by Margaret Meek are compelling and pertinent:

> *Our most pressing unsolved problem is to define and exemplify the place of children's literature in literacy.*

and

> *What the beginner reader reads makes all the difference to his/her view of reading.*

Today we see more children's books being used alongside reading materials produced especially for the classroom. Such materials have improved enormously, especially in recent years. *Collins Big Cat* is a case in point. It offers books that have the qualities of authorship and illustration of the best children's books on the market, and the kind of readability grading which helps teachers to match books to children's developing competencies, as well as built-in support for key reading strategies.

Readability grading

Over the years there have been various attempts to band, stage or level a wide range of children's books. The first edition of my own *Individualised Reading* appeared in 1973 and is still annually revised. *Book Bands for Guided Reading* (Reading Recovery UK) is the latest established guide to readability grading. The grading used within *Collins Big Cat* refers to *Book Bands*. (To match *Collins Big Cat* bands against Individualised Reading and Kaleidoscope Reading Sets, turn to the back of this book.)

What lies behind all these supports for a mix-and-match approach to reading resource provision in schools? It is because this approach leads to greater variety in the books we now find in classrooms – at best a variety which reflects the choice offered in bookshops and libraries. It supports an important principle: that children have ready access to the books they *want* to read, not those they are told they *should* read. This element of choice is vitally important in building children's independent reading habits which, if what's on offer is of sufficient quality, can create lifelong readers.

Horses' Holiday

Book-matching

Book-matching is, simply put, giving the right book to the right child. It establishes three levels of reading competence to determine which books should be used for which purposes.

Independent level = 1% miscue* or 99% accuracy
This level is useful for home reading as children can read such books on their own

Instructional level = 5–10% miscue or 90–95% accuracy
This level is useful for guided (or supported) reading

Frustration level = over 10% miscue or less than 90% accuracy
This level should always be avoided
(comprehension is below 50% at this level)

Funny Fish

Don't forget that when children are particularly interested in a story or topic, or have seen it on television, their match point can be anything up to four levels higher than usual. Similarly, for reluctant readers, allow for a corresponding drop in level.

Research in the early 1990's revealed that one of the characteristics of successful reading was the classroom provision of slightly challenging reading material. Switching to the instructional level during guided reading normally meets the slightly challenging criterion.

Book-matching solves a number of issues, firstly in relation to children who are expected to read books which they can't manage just on the basis of their age. Remember that every child has the right to be a reader from the very start and reading as late as age nine is still in the so-called "normal" range. It's my belief that no child under this age should ever be labelled "late", "delayed" or such like.

At the other extreme are children who can read before they start school. I love the story of the boy who read poetry at eighteen months. On being professionally assessed, he was said to be "unfit to commence reading instruction". The main reason such children tend to go unrecognised is that teachers don't expect their proficiency. Expect it. Imagine the effect on the self-confidence of children who can read but who are nonetheless given books that are far below their competence. What these children need is plenty of good books at the right level to interest and challenge them. Book-matching used correctly should mean that this happens.

*For this purpose, miscues are generally defined as refusals or substitutions which fail to retain the meaning of the original word

Collins Big Cat

Collins Big Cat is a reading series with a difference. That difference lies chiefly in the quality and variety of stories and non-fiction books, written and illustrated by carefully selected authors and artists who know what children love. These books are indistinguishable from the books children choose to read in bookshops and libraries, with themes of universal interest for ages four to eleven. Moreover, they are levelled into a readability sequence to support teachers working on the book-match principle, whether for guided or independent reading.

Language

We have gone to great lengths, through extensive trialling with children and teachers, to ensure that the language used in every book is as close to a child's natural language as possible, to support their developing confidence in reading and "having a go". Design and illustration have also been trialled, ensuring the books build in factors that make the act of reading more accessible and that act as a safeguard against "getting it wrong" (see *Readability* on p11). Richly patterned and highly predictable language abounds, especially in the early levels, as do rhyme and rhythm. At later levels kinds of word play are used to stimulate children's enthusiasm and enjoyment. Even the book titles themselves offer a wealth of alliteration with titles like *Bert's Band*, *Fly Facts*, *Funny Fish*, *Horses' Holiday*, *Pirate Party* and *Woody's Week*.

Fantasy story

Story genres

Collins Big Cat provides a full range of reading through different genres, from traditional tales, fantasy tales and humorous stories to rhyming stories and plays, and from non-fiction explanations and instructions to recounts and persuasive texts. This gives children a broad and exciting reading experience right from the very start.

Humorous story

Non-chronological report

Playscript

Recount of an event

Visual Literacy – 'filling the gaps'

We have also ensured that, in many cases, both the text *and* the pictures must be read in order to gain full meaning from the book. In this way, children are being encouraged to *fill the gaps*, a mark of literary quality. At the earliest levels, this means that the reader is actively involved in a rich and fulfilling plot, no matter how simple the text – look at *Fly Away Home*, for example.

Fly Away Home

The same attention to detail is given at later levels, too. Follow the sub-plot antics of the mouse in *Kind Emma*, and see how the stone cutter's face transfigures in *The Stone Cutter*.

Environmental print has been included in illustrations wherever appropriate. Look, for example, at the horse mums reading a magazine called 'Neighbours' in *Horses' Holiday*.

Non-fiction titles like *My Skateboard* prove that even at the earliest level, an imaginative and poetical text can be crafted, whilst *Let's Go to Mars* demonstrates how information can be presented in a compelling form – the book is written as a holiday brochure.

The Stone Cutter

My Skateboard

Let's Go to Mars

Reading more, mini-series and paired books

Ways to encourage children to explore different genres and read more have been built into *Collins Big Cat*. The *Reading More* section of *Ideas for Guided Reading* at the back of every book, highlights links by theme, topic, author, etc, to books in the same reading band or one higher.

Mini-series of characters occur throughout the scheme, from Tec the Detective at Red A and B bands, to Percy the Park Keeper at Yellow and Blue bands, and at the higher bands, Buzz and Bingo, and the Pet Detectives.

There are fiction and non-fiction linked themes in every band and these are indicated on the structure chart. At Blue, for example, Martin Waddell's *Bert's Band* tells a humorous tale of a marching band's misplaced consideration for others whilst *Sounds* by Julie Sykes explores everyday sounds and musical instruments.

Bert's Band

Sounds

Reading Response activity

Every *Collins Big Cat* book, fiction and non-fiction, includes a unique Reading Response activity at the end, for example a story map, a flow chart, a storyboard, a game or a poster. This has been designed to elicit and encourage the child's response to, and recall understanding of, what he or she has read. These pages offer an ideal opportunity to monitor children's understanding of the book just read.

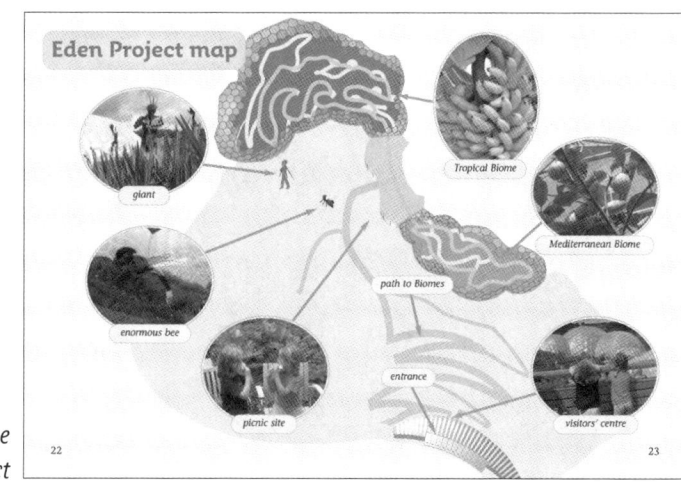

A Visit to the Eden Project

Readability

Within *Collins Big Cat*, care has been taken wherever possible to incorporate factors within the design which support the text's readability for young children. For example:

- conjunctions like *and* and *but* placed at the ends of lines to signal that there is more of the sentence to follow

- articles and their nouns not split by line-breaks

- first words of sentences appearing only at the beginning of lines

- text chunked into meaning units in the early levels

- a variety of suitable fonts at all levels so that children encounter print in different forms

- extensive use of ellipses ... to encourage anticipation and prediction (children love them!).

And finally ...

Buzz and Bingo in the Fairytale Forest

Take a look at Alan Durant's *Buzz and Bingo in the Fairytale Forest*. Buzz and his dog meet Snow White's step-mother, then Cinderella's prince, the wolf from Red Riding Hood, a boy with magical beans, a puss in boots, a brother and sister lost in the woods and still others. None of these is explicitly identified but readers know who they are. In case the reader isn't sure, the prince introduces himself as *Charming* and the wolf thinks the girl they are seeking is *delicious*. This pact between author and reader is a kind of secret they share and is a literary quality that satisfies and delights children and adults alike.

My hope is that the books in *Collins Big Cat* will be read with understanding and bring delight and excitement to young readers. Personally I'm over the Moon about them!

How to use this guide

Collins Big Cat Assessment and Support Guides provide teachers with practical planning and teaching support, helping them to assess and identify the needs of each child or group, and to teach essential literacy skills in the context of guided reading.

This guide has five main sections:

A Letter from Cliff Moon – pages 4 to 11

Collins Big Cat series editor Cliff Moon introduces *Collins Big Cat* and explains why it is such a boon to children's reading.

Structure and features – pages 12 to 23

This section outlines the content and structure of *Collins Big Cat* band 0 to 2B (Lilac to Red), including an overview of where to find what, a structure chart and further resources, including *Collins Big Cat*'s exciting CD-ROMs.

Planning and teaching – pages 24 to 67

These pages are a practical planning tool designed to help you identify quickly the right book for your guided reading groups. They provide an at-a-glance synopsis of the features of each book, including high frequency words, key learning objectives, supporting materials and curriculum links. In addition, easy-to-use two-page teaching notes giving a sample guided reading lesson are provided in the back of each *Collins Big Cat* reading book. There is also a spread detailing links to Scottish 5–14 Guidelines.

Photocopiable activity sheets – pages 68 to 127

There is a photocopiable activity sheet to accompany each of the guided reading books. These can be used to practise and extend the literacy objectives introduced in the guided reading lesson.

Collins Big Cat and guided reading – pages 128 to 144

This section provides further information on the key features of guided reading and its use within a balanced literacy programme. It also offers support in using effective assessment techniques and ideas to encourage the development of independent reading habits, for example, reading journals. There is also a full colour guide to guided reading book bands on the inside back cover.

 If you feel confident about using guided readers with your children, you could go straight to the teaching summaries on page 24.

 To learn more about *Collins Big Cat* and why it encourages the development of successful young readers, go to page 4.

 For an in-depth discussion of guided reading from ages 4 to 7, turn to page 128.

 To look at a range of assessment techniques to help you identify the needs of individuals or groups, turn to page 133.

Collins Big Cat Structure Chart: Lilac-Red B Bands

Bookband	Fiction			Paired fiction and non-fiction	
Lilac Band 0	**Cat and Dog*** Shoo Rayner 0-00-718528-6	**Goldilocks and the Three Bears** Barbara Mitchelhill 0-00-718531-6	**Get the Fruit!** Paul Shipton 0-00-718529-4	**Oh Dear Me, I'm Late for Tea** Alison Hawes 0-00-718530-8	**My Party** Maoliosa Kelly 0-00-718533-2
	The Big Turnip Monica Hughes 0-00-718644-4	**Stop That Robot!** Alison Sage 0-00-718678-9			
Pink A Band 1A	**Dinosaur Rock** Damian Harvey 0-00-718540-5	**In the Garden*** Mitch Cronick 0-00-718538-3	**The Very Wet Dog** Damian Harvey 0-00-718543-X	**The Picnic** Monica Hughes 0-00-718539-1	**Minibeasts** Siobhan Hardy 0-00-718537-5
	The Guinea Pigs Paul Shipton 0-00-718648-7	**In the Boat** Paul Shipton 0-00-718646-0			
Pink B Band 1B	**The See-saw** Paul Shipton 0-00-718553-7	**The Big Splash** Maureen Haselhurst 0-00-718557-X	**The Robot*** Paul Shipton 0-00-718546-4	**Fly Away Home** Shoo Rayner 0-00-718544-8	**The Pond** Claire Llewellyn 0-00-718549-9
	Colour Bears Tasha Pym 0-00-718652-5	**Monster Mess** Tasha Pym 0-00-718650-9			
Red A Band 2A	**A Day Out** Claire Llewellyn 0-00-718555-3	**Tec and the Hole*** Tony Mitton 0-00-718554-5	**Tec and the Cake** Tony Mitton 0-00-718545-6	**The Beach** Alison Hawes 0-00-718547-2	**Shapes on the Seashore** Frances Ridley 0-00-718556-1
	Cat and Dog Play Hide and Seek Shoo Rayner 0-00-718660-6	**Have You Ever?** Tasha Pym 0-00-718654-1			
Red B Band 2B	**Woody's Week** Michaela Morgan 0-00-718560-X	**Pirates*** Paul Shipton 0-00-718561-8	**Where is the Wind?** Celia Warren 0-00-718566-9	**Tec and the Litter** Tony Mitton 0-00-718565-0	**At the Dump** Claire Llewellyn 0-00-718563-4
	What's For Breakfast? Paul Shipton 0-00-718668-1	**Super Ben** Steve Smallman 0-00-718656-8			

*available as a Talking Book on the CD-ROM

Non-fiction

Stripes
Monica Hughes
0-00-718534-0

Carry Me
Monica Hughes
0-00-718535-9

Look Out Butterfly!*
Nic Bishop
0-00-718532-4

How to Make a Scarecrow
Kim Wilde
0-00-718645-2

What am I?
Maoliosa Kelly
0-00-718679-7

Cars
Monica Hughes
0-00-718558-8

Pushing and Pulling
Monica Hughes
0-00-718541-3

My Skateboard*
Maoliosa Kelly
0-00-718536-7

Shapes
Monica Hughes
0-00-718649-5

How Many Animals?
Lee Newman
0-00-718647-9

Wheels
Frances Ridley
0-00-718550-2

Come to the Circus!
Damian Harvey
0-00-718551-0

Cats*
Claire Llewellyn
0-00-718548-0

We Like Fruit
Gill Budgell
0-00-7186-53-3

I Can Do It!
Paul Shipton
0-00-718651-7

Up, Up and Away
Sue Graves
0-00-718559-6

What's Inside?
Monica Hughes
0-00-718542-1

In the Dark*
Claire Llewellyn
0-00-718552-9

My Bike Ride
Maoliosa Kelly
0-00-718661-4

Weather Report
Alison Hawes
0-00-718655-X

What Do You Like?
Anna Owen
0-00-718564-2

Let's Go Shopping
Betty Moon
0-00-718567-7

The Oak Tree*
Anna Owen
0-00-718562-6

My Exercise Diary
Alison Hawes
0-00-718669-X

What Are You Making?
Alison Hawes
978-0-00-718657-6

ICT resources

CD-ROM A
0-00-719865-5

Other teaching resources

Big Book of Rhymes A
0-00-718932-X

Big Book of Non-fiction A
0-00-718933-8

Assessment and Support Guide A
0-00-718928-1

Resource and Records Manager CD-ROM
0-00-720080-3

Features of *Collins Big Cat* Guided Reading Books

Collins Big Cat offers exciting reads designed to capture children's imagination, entertain them and encourage them to love reading. As children read *Collins Big Cat* books, they will benefit from the following features:

Wide range of genres

Collins Big Cat offers an equal split between fiction and non-fiction books and a wide variety of genres and text types – e.g. humorous stories, traditional stories, rhyming stories, non-chronological reports and recounts. At each level is a pair of fiction and non-fiction books on related themes, enabling teachers to link easily across genres.

Top authors

The books – fiction and non-fiction – are written by a range of outstanding children's authors. These include Michael Morpurgo, Julia Donaldson, Nick Butterworth, Ian Whybrow, Alan Durant, Rose Impey, Martin Waddell, Tony Mitton and Julia Jarman. Top quality texts make reading enjoyable for a child, which is a huge stimulus to learn.

Rich illustrations

Collins Big Cat books are illustrated by leading children's illustrators, including Nick Butterworth, Shoo Rayner, Ainslie McLeod and outstanding photographers such as Nic Bishop and Jonathan and Angela Scott. Each book is highly visual with a strong narrative in the pictures which can be used to develop visual literacy and oral retelling.

Horses' Holiday

Speaking and listening

Collins Big Cat has been specifically developed to encourage children's speaking and listening skills as well as their reading skills, by including strong visual plots. In the early books (Pink A – Red B), the left hand page provides simple, supported text for the child to read, while the right hand pages extend the story, encouraging children to tell the story in their own words. This enables children from the very earliest stages to be involved in an exciting reading experience, using a wider, richer vocabulary and more complex language than they are able to read as text.

Simple text describes what is happening in the picture, and provides opportunity to identify high frequency words.

Fly Away Home

Ladybird is on the tree.

2

3

Interest words are picture-cued to help with prediction.

The picture on the facing page develops the plot and shows what happens next, engaging children and allowing them to tell the story in their own words, using richer vocabulary and more complex language.

The caterpillars and insects lived on the tree and they didn't want the ladybird to be there. They chased the ladybird away.

Reading response pages

Each book has a unique reading response activity at the end of it. This enables the teacher to check each child's comprehension through speaking and listening in response to the spread. The wide range of activities, from storyboards to flow charts to maps to glossaries, are ideal supports for recapping, retelling and revisiting the main events in the book, as well as linking to activity work outside the guided reading session.

Fly Away Home

The picture enables the child to retell the story. It develops children's visual literacy skills.

Collins Big Cat book bands

Collins Big Cat is clearly structured into 20 bands based on the Institute of Education's Guided Reading Book Bands, and is both easy to use by itself, or to slot in alongside existing resources for guided reading. For more information on the bands, turn to the full colour chart on the inside back cover.

Colour coded levels help you match Big Cat to Book Bands for Guided Reading and help you match the children's ability level to Collins Big Cat levels.

Ideas for guided reading at your fingertips

At the back of every Big Cat guided reading book is a double-page spread of *Ideas for guided reading*. These are provided in every *Collins Big Cat* book so they are right at your fingertips during guided reading lessons, and there's no need to use a different edition to the children. *Ideas for guided reading* give you a range of useful information as well as outlining the most effective way to use the book in a guided reading session.

Learning objectives
Helps you plan learning objectives, based on PNS Framework, NLS Framework and PiPs Playing with sounds and QCA Speaking, Listening, Learning Objectives.

Curriculum links
Enables you to link the reading to other areas of the school curriculum.

High frequency words
Helps you monitor the child's acquisition of high frequency words.

Interest words
Gives you at a glance the interest words children will tackle when reading this book.

Returning to the book
Recapping and reviewing the text and learning objectives, with support of the Reading Response pages at the end of the book.

Fly Away Home

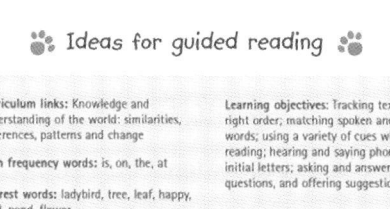

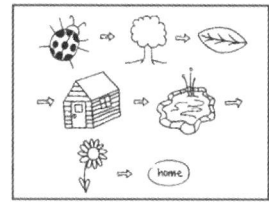

Getting started
Ideas and activities to introduce the book and learning objectives.

Reading and responding
Ideas to support the groups independent reading of the book, prompting the children to problem solve as they read and to predict what might happen next.

Checking and moving on
Ideas and activities for group, paired or independent work arising from the guided reading, including a visual literacy sketch idea.

Reading more
This suggests another book the children can read at the same or next reading level, related by subject, author or genre.

At-a-glance information to help teachers plan their guided reading lesson.

Collins Big Cat electronic texts

Electronic texts are a vital part of children's reading and writing experience today, both in education and in everyday life, from the Internet to mobile phone texting. Skill in a variety of text types, including electronic, is key to the development of successful literacy.

Every day information comes from electronic sources such as:
- CD-ROMs
- the Internet
- computer and video games
- e-mail
- mobile phone texting
- TV text services
- TV
- video
- DVD
- radio

For children to use these sources effectively, they will need to develop a set of literacy skills specifically aimed at electronic media.

Collins Big Cat interactive resources

Collins Big Cat provides a range of interactive resources that strengthen the development of these new literacies. They are designed to be used in conjunction with the printed books by children working in groups or pairs. They can also be used in shared work with the whole class, using an interactive whiteboard, PC, or projector and screen.

Collins Big Cat CD-ROMs A, *B* and *C* provide:
- talking books
- active books
- electronic Big Books
- ClipArt library
- book review

Collins Big Cat Talking Books

The talking books provide electronic versions of selected Big Cat books, one fiction and one non-fiction, from each reading band. They give children the opportunity to:
- listen to the story as it's read aloud on screen
- 'read along' to the audio, following the pictures and text on screen
- read the text on screen without audio support
- check each word individually with an audio prompt
- follow up with a range of interactive activities.

Animation and sound effects support comprehension and enhance the text by engaging the reader. The talking books are entirely suitable for use in guided reading sessions but they have been designed so that children can also use them independently without adult intervention.

Children can track the text as it is read aloud.

Children can check each word by clicking on it.

Sound effects can be turned on and off.

It wasn't much fun down on the farm.

Good Fun Farm

Mooo!

Grunt!

Good Fun Farm

The vibrant illustrations are animated to engage the reader.

Page 1

Children can page through the book by clicking on the forward and back arrows.

Children can jump to different parts of the book using the navigation slider.

Good Fun Farm Talking Book

Talking book interactive activities

The talking books are followed by up to three interactive activities that relate to text, word and sentence level learning objectives from the text and support exploration. The activities correspond with the level of the books.

Activity 1: Sequencing
Children are asked to sequence randomly arranged pictures from the book to retell the story in order to check their understanding.

Children simply drag and drop the pictures into the right order.

This activity can be extended into a free writing opportunity, where pupils write about each of the pictures in the sequence, telling their own story.

Children can check their answer and receive instant feedback.

If the wrong answer is given for a third time, the pictures animate to show the correct sequence.

Activity 2: Matching
Depending on the level of the book, children are asked to match pictures, words or sentences to reinforce understanding and reading of the text.

Children select the picture, word or sentence that matches the picture by clicking on it. There are five matching tasks in each activity.

Images, words and sentences are randomly chosen from a bank, so the activity can be revisited. Children can check their answer and receive instant feedback.

Activity 3: Sentence building and free writing
Children are given a picture from the book and asked to choose words from a word bank to complete sentences about it.

Pupils drag and drop word tiles into the correct sequence to form a sentence.

At early levels, pupils drag missing words into gaps in the sentence. Pupils can check their answer and receive instant feedback.

An extension of this activity allows children a free writing option to support extended writing.

Children can use the bank of words and punctuation as a starting point for their free writing.

The words and punctuation are inserted into the text box by clicking on the tiles.

The illustration and text are printed together on a single sheet of paper.

Collins Big Cat Active Books

Each CD-ROM contains one Active Book. These books are designed as interactive electronic texts – they could not exist on paper due to their interactive nature. They provide children with the opportunity to influence the development of a story, making choices and determining outcomes.

The reader chooses how to navigate the book in order to build their own story, carry out their own

investigation or create their own report. The level of complexity is appropriate to each age group.

By the end of each active book, the child will have created their own unique story which they can 'publish' for print or electronic presentation to the rest of the class, using the save and replay facility.

Each active book is:
- interactive – requiring an active reader response to move on
- non-linear – so that the sequencing can be varied
- multimedia – involving text, sound and animation.

Each active book links to themes and storylines explored in some of the printed Big Cat books at that level.

On CD-ROM A, the active book is *Big Cat's Party*. It's Big Cat's birthday and he is having a party. The reader is asked to make a number of choices, including which characters help Big Cat on the way to the party. The story features popular nursery rhymes and their characters.

The active book is linked to *Oh Dear Me, I'm Late for Tea!* (Lilac/Band 0), *My Party* (Lilac/Band 0), *The Beach* (Red A/Band 2A) and *Big Book of Rhyme A* featuring a collection of nursery rhymes.

Electronic Big Books

Each CD provides an electronic version of the *Collins Big Cat* Big Books. These are ideal for:
- whole class/group work
- use with an interactive whiteboard
- generating group discussion
- use in plenary sessions.

Collins Big Cat ClipArt library

Each CD-ROM contains a collection of ClipArt of characters and objects from the books, ideal for:
- customizing worksheets, record sheets and own work
- making models
- creating multimedia presentations.

Big Cat's Party Active Book

Collins Big Cat book review

This downloadable form for the reader to fill in is designed to be used by children as a personal record of their own reading. It supports:

- personal reviews
- objective understanding of the elements of a book
- critical appraisal of books read.

Collins Big Cat resource and records managers

The powerful resource manager tool is designed to help teachers find just the right guided reading title quickly and easily by using search facilities within a database.

There is a searchable database of the whole *Collins Big Cat* series.

Collins Big Cat Big Books

The four *Collins Big Cat* Big Books provide an ideal accompaniment to the guided reading books. They are designed to be used in the whole class shared reading and teaching sessions which precede guided reading in the literacy hour. They provide opportunities to introduce a particular subject, genre or a teaching point prior to group guided reading.

There are four *Collins Big Cat* Big Books. The *Big Books of Rhymes A* and *B* are anthologies of carefully selected poems and rhymes – these are mostly new and original from a wide range of well-known children's poets. These provide exciting opportunities for the children to enjoy whole class reading with colourfully illustrated and often humorous rhymes which will allow the teacher to teach and the whole class to practise

Each book has a dedicated book information screen, listing the themes and learning objectives covered by the book. All book information can be edited and updated by the user.

When new titles appear in the series, the database can be easily updated through a link to the *Collins Big Cat* website.

The records manager provides a reading record template for teachers to use in creating running records for each child's assessment. It is:

- simple to complete
- fully editable
- individualized.

Big Book of Rhymes A

crucial reading skills. This might be one-to-one matching, word attack strategies as well as specific objectives related to the particular text. Many of the rhymes are linked by theme to the Big Cat guided reading stories, and so can be used to introduce a particular subject prior to reading the book.

The *Big Books of Non-fiction* provide distinctive non-fiction text types, so children can be introduced to non-fiction and how it is so different from fiction. A number of non-fiction text features are provided in order to make this point – e.g. diagrams, photographs, labels, captions etc. Again, there are some thematic links with the guided reading texts.

Collins Big Cat Lilac-Red B books

This Guide contains book-by-book details and planning notes for all *Collins Big Cat* guided reading books from book bands Lilac to Red B.

This page directs you to the right page for information and PCMs for all the Lilac to Red B guided reading books. To find a short text summary, learning objectives, high frequency words and related resources for a particular guided reading book, look at the page number next to 'Info'. To find the PCM for the particular book, look at the number next to 'PCM'. The PCMs are numbered 1 to 60 and they start on page 68.

Lilac / Band 0

Cat and Dog	Goldilocks and the Three Bears	Get the Fruit!	Oh Dear Me, I'm Late for Tea!	My Party	Stripes
Fiction		Fiction	Fiction	Non-fiction	Non-fiction
Info p26 PCM 1	Fiction	Info p26 PCM 3	Info p28 PCM 4	Info p28 PCM 5	Info p28 PCM 6
A wordless story with a predictable structure	Info p26 PCM 2	A wordless story with a predictable structure	A wordless story with a predictable structure	A wordless non-fiction book	A wordless non-fiction book
	A wordless traditional story				

Carry Me	Look Out Butterfly!	The Big Turnip	How to Make a Scarecrow	Stop that Robot!	What am I?
Non-fiction	Non-fiction	Fiction	Non-fiction	Fiction	Non-fiction
Info p30 PCM 7	Info p30 PCM 8	Info p30 PCM 9	Info p32 PCM 10	Info p32 PCM 11	Info p32 PCM 12
A wordless non-fiction book	A wordless non-fiction book	A wordless traditional story	A wordless instruction text	A wordless fantasy story	An information book

Pink A / Band 1A

In the Garden	The Very Wet Dog	Dinosaur Rock	The Picnic	Minibeasts	Cars
Fiction	Fiction	Fiction	Fiction	Non-fiction	Non-fiction
Info p34 PCM 13	Info p34 PCM 14	Info p34 PCM 15	Info p36 PCM 16	Info p36 PCM 17	Info p36 PCM 18
A story with predictable structure and patterned language	A story with predictable structure and patterned language	A story with predictable structure and patterned language	A wordless story with a predictable structure	A simple information book	A non-fiction report

Pushing and Pulling	My Skateboard	The Guinea Pigs	Shapes	In the Boat	How Many Animals?
Non-fiction	Non-fiction	Fiction	Non-fiction	Fiction	Non-fiction
Info p38 PCM 19	Info p38 PCM 20	Info p38 PCM 21	Info p40 PCM 22	Info p40 PCM 23	Info p40 PCM 24
A simple non-fiction recount	A simple non-fiction recount	A story with predictable structure and patterned language	A simple non-fiction book	A story with predictable structure and patterned language	A simple information book

Pink B / Band 1B

The See-saw	The Big Splash!	The Robot	Fly Away Home	The Pond	Wheels
Fiction	Fiction	Fiction	Fiction	Non-fiction	Non-fiction
Info p42 PCM 25	Info p42 PCM 26	Info p42 PCM 27	Info p44 PCM 28	Info p44 PCM 29	Info p44 PCM 30
A story with predictable structure and patterned language	A story with predictable structure and patterned language	A story with predictable structure and patterned language	A story with predictable structure and patterned language	A simple non-fiction report	A simple non-fiction book

Come to the Circus!	Cats	Colour Bears	We Like Fruit	Monster Mess	I Can Do It!
Non-fiction	Fiction	Fiction	Non-fiction	Fiction	Non-fiction
Info p46 PCM 31	Info p46 PCM 32	Info p46 PCM 33	Info p48 PCM 34	Info p48 PCM 35	Info p48 PCM 36
A simple information book	A non-fiction report	A story with predictable structure and patterned language	A non-fiction report	A story with predictable structure and patterned language	A simple information book

Red A / Band 2A

A Day Out	Tec and the Cake	Tec and the Hole	The Beach	Shapes on the Seashore	What's Inside?
Fiction	Fiction	Fiction	Fiction	Non-fiction	Non-fiction
Info p50 PCM 37	Info p50 PCM 38	Info p50 PCM 39	Info p52 PCM 40	Info p52 PCM 41	Info p52 PCM 42
A story with predictable structure and patterned language	A story with predictable structure and patterned language	A story with predictable structure and patterned language	A story with predictable structure and patterned language	A simple non-fiction recount	A simple information book

In the Dark	Up, Up and Away	Cat and Dog Play Hide and Seek	My Bike Ride	Have You Ever?	Weather Report
Non-fiction	Non-fiction	Fiction	Non-fiction	Fiction	Non-fiction
Info p54 PCM 43	Info p54 PCM 44	Info p54 PCM 45	Info p56 PCM 46	Info p56 PCM 47	Info p56 PCM 48
A simple non-fiction recount	A simple non-fiction recount	A story with predictable structure and patterned language	A simple non-fiction recount	A story with predictable structure and patterned language	A non-fiction report

Red B / Band 2B

Pirates	Where is the Wind?	Woody's Week	Tec and the Litter	At the Dump	What Do You Like?
Fiction	Fiction	Fiction	Fiction	Non-fiction	Non-fiction
Info p58 PCM 49	Info p58 PCM 50	Info p58 PCM 51	Info p60 PCM 52	Info p60 PCM 53	Info p60 PCM 54
A story with predictable structure and patterned language	A story with predictable structure and patterned language	A story with predictable structure and patterned language	A story with predictable structure and patterned language	A simple non-fiction recount	A simple non-fiction recount

Let's Go Shopping!	The Oak Tree	What's For Breakfast?	My Exercise Diary	Super Ben	What Are You Making?
Non-fiction	Non-fiction	Fiction	Non-fiction	Fiction	Non-fiction
Info p62 PCM 55	Info p62 PCM 56	Info p62 PCM 57	Info p64 PCM 58	Info p64 PCM 59	Info p64 PCM 60
A simple non-fiction report	A simple non-chronological report	A story with predictable structure and patterned language	A simple non-fiction recount	A patterned story with predictable structure	A non-fiction recount

Book band	About the book	Text type	Curriculum links

Cat and Dog

Shoo Rayner

A wordless picture story about two animals. Cat steps out through the cat flap, unaware that Dog is about to pounce. A frantic chase follows, which almost ends in catastrophe. But there is a surprise twist in the tale when Dog rescues Cat. The final spread shows the route of Cat and Dog's chase through the park and can be used by the children to discuss and retell the story. Shoo Rayner also wrote and illustrated the Pink B story *Fly Away Home*.

A wordless story with a predictable structure

Early Learning Goals: Knowledge and understanding of the world: Find out about some features of living things

Lilac / Band 0

Goldilocks and the Three Bears

Barbara Mitchelhill and Michelle Mathers

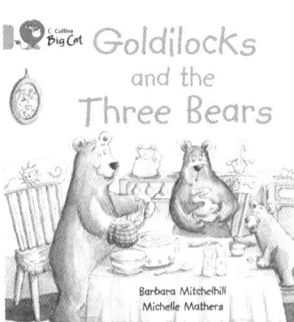

A wordless picture story, retelling the traditional tale of Goldilocks and the Three Bears. The story follows Goldilocks' journey through the bears' house, as she samples their bowls of porridge, and tries out their three differently-sized chairs and beds. When Goldilocks is discovered sleeping in Baby Bear's bed, however, the story takes a different twist and Goldilocks is invited to join the bears for breakfast. The story map on pages 14 and 15 gives children the opportunity to recap the story.

A wordless traditional story

Early Learning Goals: Communication, language and literacy: Respond to and make up their own stories; Retell narratives in the correct sequence Mathematical development: Exploring comparison words

Lilac / Band 0

Get the Fruit!

Paul Shipton and Trevor Dunton

A humorous picture story set in the jungle. A pair of monkeys have their eye on a juicy-looking fruit hanging just out of reach. The wordless story follows their inventive but unsuccessful individual attempts to grab the tempting fruit. Finally, the monkeys succeed. But was the effort worth it? A storyboard on pages 14–15 provides an opportunity for children to retell the story in their own words.

A wordless story with a predictable structure

Early Learning Goals: Communication, Language and Literacy: Use language to imagine and recreate roles and experience Mathematical development: Use ideas to solve practical problems

Lilac / Band 0

Learning objectives	High frequency words	Interest words	Related resources
NLS Framework Objectives YR T1C: Understand and use correctly terms about books and print; T1D: Track the book in the right order, page by page, left to right, top to bottom; pointing while reading/telling a story; T5: To use some formal elements when retelling stories. *Speaking, Listening, Learning objective* *ELG* Communication, language and literacy: Use talk to organise, sequence and clarify thinking, ideas feeling and events *Scottish 5–14 Strands:* Listening, Talking, Reading, Writing, Level A	wordless book	cat, dog	*Big Book of Non-fiction A*: pp22–23 'Lauren's school day', supports work on tracking and sequencing the main events of a story or non-fiction recount. **PCM 1**: Children can cut out and sequence parts of the story. **CD-ROM A**: *Cat and Dog* is also a Talking Book. It includes three related activities and an opportunity for free writing.
NLS Framework Objectives YR T5: Understand how story book language works and to use when re-telling stories; T7: Use knowledge of familiar texts to re-enact or re-tell to others, with main points in correct sequence; W10: Learn new words from their reading and shared experiences. *PiPs Playing with Sounds* Step 1: Explore sound effects using a variety of instruments when re-telling story *Speaking, Listening, Learning objective* Y1 T1 Drama 4: Explore familiar themes and characters through role-play *Scottish 5–14 Strands:* Listening, Talking, Reading, Writing, Level A	wordless book	Goldilocks, three, bears	**PCM 2**: Children can cut out and sequence key events of the story.
NLS Framework Objectives YR T1C: Understand and use correctly terms about books and print; T9: Be aware of story structures, e.g. actions/ reactions, consequences; W10: Collect new words from their reading and shared experiences; W11: Make collections of personal interest or significant words… *Speaking, Listening, Learning objective* *ELG* Communication, language and literacy: Use talk to organise, sequence and clarify thinking, ideas feeling and events *Scottish 5–14 Strands:* Listening, Talking, Reading, Writing, Level A	wordless book	fruit	*Big Book of Rhymes A*: p4 'Hippo! Hippo!' supports work on the theme of solving problems. **PCM 3**: Children can draw the middle stage of the sequence.

Book band	About the book	Text type	Curriculum links

Lilac / Band 0

Oh Dear Me, I'm Late for Tea!

Alison Hawes and Mike Phillips

A wordless picture story following Granny's race against the clock, as she has just one hour to reach her destination. The story shows Granny's imaginative modes of transport, before revealing why she is in such a hurry. Pages 14 and 15 show Granny's pictorial recount of the different transport she used. This story is paired with a non-fiction book on the same theme: *My Party* by Maoliosa Kelly.	A wordless story with a predictable structure	*Early Learning Goals:* Creative Development: Use their imagination in role play and stories; Knowledge and understanding of the world: Find out about objects they observe

Lilac / Band 0

My Party

Maoliosa Kelly and Steve Lumb

A wordless picture book about a birthday party. The photographs provide a window on all the preparations, the birthday tea, the guests arriving at the party, the gifts and the games. Pages 14 and 15 show the different stages of the party and preparations in a sequenced flow-diagram. This non-fiction book is paired with a story on a similar theme: *Oh Dear Me I'm Late for Tea* by Alison Hawes.	Wordless non-fiction book	*Early Learning Goals:* Personal, social and emotional development: be confident to try new activities and speak to a familiar group

Lilac / Band 0

Stripes

Monica Hughes

A non-fiction picture book that takes a photographic look at all sorts of stripes in the environment. Alongside each photograph is a close-up snapshot that magnifies the various textiles and materials in detail. These images are repeated on pages 14 and 15 for children to try to recall where each set of stripes comes from.	A wordless non-fiction book	*Early Learning Goals:* Knowledge and understanding of the world: Investigate objects and materials using all the senses; look at similarities, differences, patterns and change; find out about living things and the features of place they live

Learning objectives	High frequency words	Interest words	Related resources
NLS Framework Objectives YR T1C: To understand and use correctly terms about books and print; T7: Using knowledge of familiar texts to re-enact or re-tell to others; S3: Understanding that books are ordered left to right and need to be read that way to make sense; W10: Learning new words from their shared experiences. *Speaking and Listening objective* ELG Communication, language and literacy: Use talk to organise, sequence and clarify thinking, ideas, feeling and events *Scottish 5–14 Strands:* Listening, Talking, Reading, Writing, Level A	wordless book	wordless book	**PCM 4**: Children can make up two more appointments that Granny is late for and complete the sentences.
NLS Framework Objectives YR T2 Use a variety of cues when reading: knowledge of the story and its context, awareness of grammatical sense; T7 Use knowledge of the text to re-enact or retell, recounting the main points in sequence and key themes. *Speaking and listening objectives* ELG Communication, language and literacy: Use language to imagine and recreate roles and experiences; Use talk to organise, sequence and clarify thinking and idea. *Scottish 5–14 Strands:* Listening, Talking, Reading, Writing, Level A	wordless book	party	*Big Book of Non-fiction B*: pp6–7 'Dotty Dog' supports the theme of parties. **PCM 5**: Children cut out and sequence the different stages of the party.
NLS Framework Objectives YR T1c Track the text in the right order, page by page, left to right, top to bottom; T7 Use knowledge of the text to re-tell to others, identifying key themes and sequencing main points; T8 Locate significant parts of the text using photographs. *Speaking and Listening objective* *ELG* Communication, language and literacy: Interact with others, negotiating and taking turns; Using talk to imagine and recreate roles and experience. *Scottish 5–14 Strands:* Listening, Talking, Reading, Writing, Level A	wordless book	stripes	**PCM 6**: Children add stripes to the pictures, and read the captions, before drawing a picture and completing a caption of their own.

Book band	About the book	Text type	Curriculum links

Lilac / Band 0

Carry Me

Monica Hughes

A wordless picture book showing how different animals carry their young. Readers will discover, through a series of photographs, that some animals carry their young by the teeth, some on their backs and others in a special pouch. Photographs of all the animal babies (and a human baby!) included in the book are repeated on pages 14 and 15.

A wordless non-fiction book

Early Learning Goals: Knowledge and understanding of the world: Finding out about living things

---

Lilac / Band 0

Look Out, Butterfly!

Nic Bishop

A wordless non-fiction book, told through brightly coloured photographs. It traces a butterfly's trail from one flower to another. The narrative is predictable but, look out! Butterfly almost lands on a yellow flower where a camouflaged crab spider waits to pounce! A story map on pages 14 and 15 retells the story through repeated photographs.

A wordless non-fiction book

Early Learning Goals: Mathematical development: Use everyday words to describe position; Knowledge and understanding of the world: Find out about and identify features of living things

---

Lilac / Band 0

The Big Turnip

Monica Hughes and Lisa Williams

The traditional story of *The Enormous Turnip* is retold through humorous illustrations. The structure of this wordless text shows clearly how a story is built up through a series of events. The story ending reminds the reader that cooperation is often the best way to achieve a result! A storyboard on pages 14 and 15 shows the sequence of events in six numbered stages.

A wordless traditional story

Early Learning Goals: Communication, Language and Literacy: Respond to and make up own stories; re-tell narratives in the correct sequence; Mathematical Development: Use language of comparisons

Learning objectives	High frequency words	Interest words	Related resources
NLS Framework Objectives YR T1d Track the text in the right order, page by page, left to right, top to bottom, pointing while reading, making one-to-one matches; T7 Use knowledge of the text to re-tell to others, identifying key themes and sequencing main points; T8 Locate significant parts of the text, using photographs. *Speaking and Listening objective* *ELG* Communication, language and literacy: Speak clearly and audibly with control and show awareness of the listener *Scottish 5–14 Strands:* Listening, Talking, Reading, Writing, Level A	wordless book	carry	**PCM 7**: Children can match up animals and their young.
NLS Framework Objectives YR T7 Use knowledge of familiar texts to re-enact or re-tell to others; T1c Understand and use correctly terms about books and print, e.g. book, cover, title; T1d Track the text in the right order, page by page, left to right, top to bottom. *Speaking and Listening objective* *ELG:* Communication, Language and Literacy: Use talk to organise ideas *Scottish 5–14 Strands:* Listening, Talking, Reading, Writing, Level A	wordless book	butterfly	*Big Book of Rhymes A*: pp 8–9 'Caterpillar, Caterpillar' also explores the topic of butterflies **PCM 8**: Children can retell the butterfly's journey. **CD-ROM A**: *Look Out, Butterfly!* is a Talking Book. It includes three related activities and an opportunity for free writing.
Primary Framework objectives Foundation Stage Understanding and interpreting texts: Re-tell narratives in the correct sequence, drawing on the language patterns of stories. Engaging with and responding to texts: Show an understanding of the elements of stories, such as main character, sequence of events, and openings. *Primary Framework objectives Year 1* Speaking: Re-tell stories, ordering events using story language. *Scottish 5–14 Strands:* Listening, Talking, Reading, Writing, Level A	wordless book	big, turnip	**PCM 9** features six illustrations from the story for children to cut out and sequence. The pictures can then be used to re-tell the story to a partner or to make into a storybook.

Book band	About the book	Text type	Curriculum links

Lilac / Band 0

How to Make a Scarecrow

Kim Wilde

A wordless instruction text by a celebrity gardener that combines photographs and illustrations to show how a scarecrow is made using recycled materials. Each step of the construction process is clearly depicted, in sequence, concluding with a photograph of the finished model. The process is summarised in a flow diagram on pages 14 and 15.

A wordless instruction text

Early Learning Goals: Knowledge and Understanding of the World; Creative Development

---

Lilac / Band 0

Stop that Robot!

Alison Sage and Gary Dunn

Every child's dream; a robot that tidies your room! But in this wordless picture book, the advantage-taking boy discovers his wised-up robot messing everything up again! Hiding the mess, the boy goes out to play … before all is revealed and Mum turns to the robot herself. Pages 14 and 15 provide a story map for children to retell the story in their own words.

A wordless fantasy story

Early Learning Goals: PHSE: Feelings

Lilac / Band 0

What am I?

Maoliosa Kelly, Antony Elworthy and Beccy Blake

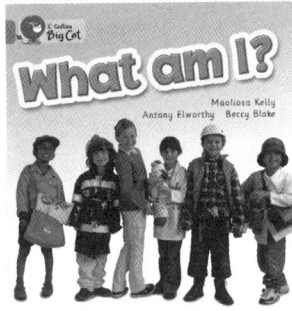

This wordless non-fiction book looks at different types of work that adults do. Photographs show children dressed up with the appropriate props, while the illustrations reveal a range of typical activities for each job. The professions covered are: doctor, vet, teacher, postman, builder and firewoman. The photographs of the dressed-up children repeated on pages 14–15 give children another opportunity to discuss "What Am I?"

An information book

Early Learning Goals: Communication, Language and Literac Use language to imagine and recreate roles and experiences Knowledge and Understanding of the World: Find out abou events in the lives of people they know. Creative Developmen Use imagination in role play.

Learning objectives	High frequency words	Interest words	Related resources
Primary Framework objectives Foundation Stage Engaging with and responding to texts: Show an understanding of how information can be found in non-fiction texts to answer questions about where, who, why and how. Word recognition: Read and write one grapheme for each of the 44 phonemes. Group discussion and interaction: Use talk to organise, sequence and clarify thinking, ideas, feelings and events. *Scottish 5–14 Strands:* Listening, Talking, Reading, Writing, Level A	wordless book	scarecrow	**PCM 10** is a planning sheet for children to design their own scarecrow. They can select materials from the list of suggested resources and draw a picture to show how their finished model will look.
Primary Framework objectives Foundation Stage Understanding and interpreting texts: Show an understanding of the elements of stories, such as main character, sequence of events, and openings; Retell narratives in the correct sequence, drawing on the language patterns of stories. Speaking/Group discussion and interaction: Use talk to organise, sequence and clarify thinking, ideas, feelings and events. Speaking/Drama/Engaging with and responding to texts: Use language to imagine and recreate roles and experiences. *Scottish 5–14 Strands:* Listening, Talking, Reading, Writing, Level A	wordless book	stop, that, robot	**PCM 11**: Children cut out six illustrations reproduced from the book and arrange them in the sequence of the story.
Primary Framework objectives Foundation Stage Understanding and interpreting texts: Show an understanding of the elements of stories, such as main character, sequence of events, and openings, and how information can be found in non-fiction texts to answer question about where, who, why and how. Speaking/Drama/Engaging with and responding to texts: Use language to imagine and recreate roles and experiences. Word recognition: decoding (reading) and encoding (spelling): Read a range of familiar and common words and simple sentences independently. *Scottish 5–14 Strands:* Listening, Talking, Reading, Writing, Level A	wordless book	what, am, I	**PCM 12**: Children match people to the work that they do.

Book band	About the book	Text type	Curriculum links

In the Garden

Mitch Cronick and Melanie Sharp

A simple story about two boys and the different places they find to play in as they explore a garden. They travel from the tent, to the sandpit, through the grass, the leaves and the mud before finally ending up in the bath. A story map on pages 14 and 15 shows the trail the boys make.

A story with predictable structure and patterned language

Early Learning Goals Personal Social and Emotional Development: Respond to experiences, showing a range of feelings where appropriate; Knowledge and understanding of the world: Finding out about their environment

Pink A / Band 1A

The Very Wet Dog

Damian Harvey and Francois Hall

A humorous picture story about a dog's day out with a girl and her Dad. It's a lovely day for walking in the park. Before long, the dog is chasing a duck through the mud, and dragging its owner into mud and a pond. The dog is taken home, shakes water all over the car and Dad, and at home gets hosed down in the garden – along with poor Dad! Children can follow the dog's journey using the story map on pages 14 and 15.

A story with a predictable structure and patterned language

Early Learning Goals: Personal Social and Emotional Development: Respond to experiences, showing a range of feelings

Pink A / Band 1A

Dinosaur Rock

Damian Harvey and Matt Ward

A simple picture story about a band of dinosaurs and the instruments they all play: guitars, trumpets, drums, flutes, pianos. The dinosaurs build up slowly into a huge band until finally they start to rock. A story map on pages 14 and 15 lets children recap and discuss the story.

Story with predictable structure and patterned language

Early Learning Goals: Creative development (music): Recognise sounds, simple songs and sound patterns

Pink A / Band 1A

Learning objectives	High frequency words	Interest words	Related resources
NLS Framework Objectives YR T5 Understand storybook language and use some formal elements when re-telling a story; T9 Awareness of story structure, e.g. actions / reactions, consequences, build up and conclusion of story; W5 Reading on sight a range of familiar words. *Early Learning Goal* Communication, language and literacy: Show understanding of story elements, e.g. characters, sequence of events. *Speaking and listening objective:* *ELG:* Communication, Language and Literacy: Use talk to organise, sequence and clarify thinking and ideas. *Scottish 5–14 Strands:* Listening, Talking, Reading, Writing, Level A	in, the	grass, leaves, sandpit, mud, tent, bath	*Big Book of Non-fiction B*: pp 14–22 'A Year in Aidan's Garden' links to the theme of a family garden. **PCM 13** is a writing frame for children to retell the story using interest words. **CD-ROM A**: *In the Garden* is a Talking Book. It includes three related activities and an opportunity for free writing.
NLS Framework Objectives YR T1d: Track the text in the right order, page by page, left to right, top to bottom, pointing while reading, and making one-to-one correspondences. T4: Notice the difference between spoken and written forms through re-telling known stories; W2a: Hearing and saying phonemes in initial letters. *Early Learning Goal:* Communication, Language and Literacy: Retell narratives in the correct sequence. *Speaking and listening objective* ELG Communication, Language and Literacy: Use language to imagine and recreate roles and experiences *Scottish 5–14 Strands:* Listening, Talking, Reading, Writing, Level A	in, the	car, park, mud, pond, house, garden	**PCM 14**: Children fill in the words to retell the story.
NLS Framework Objectives YR: T2 Use a variety of cues when reading: knowledge of the story and its context, and awareness of grammatical sense. S3 Know that words are ordered from left to right and need to be read that way; *PiPs Playing with Sounds* Steps 2, 3 and 4: Know phoneme-grapheme correspondences: t, g, d, f, p. *Speaking, Listening, Learning teaching objectives* Y1 T1 Drama 4 Explore familiar themes and character through improvisation and role-play *Scottish 5–14 Strands:* Listening, Talking, Reading, Writing, Level A	they, play	dinosaur, rock, guitars, trumpets, drums, flutes, pianos, all	**PCM 15**: Children match the labels with the dinosaur's instruments.

Book band	About the book	Text type	Curriculum links

Pink A / Band 1A

The Picnic

Monica Hughes and Gustavo Mazali

This simple picture book with a familiar theme, looks at the different things that a family take on a picnic: the rug, the basket, the sandwiches, the cakes and the drinks. The scene is set for a perfect picnic, until the wasps arrive! A labelled illustration on pages 14 and 15 gives children the chance to recount and discuss the story. This story is paired with an information book with a similar theme: *Minibeasts* by Siobhan Hardy.

A story with a predictable structure and patterned language

Early Learning Goals: Personal Social and Emotional Development: Respond to experiences, showing a range of feelings

Pink A / Band 1A

Minibeasts

Siobhan Hardy and Steve Lumb

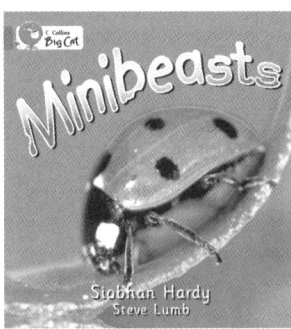

The brightly coloured photographs in this picture book show common minibeasts that most children will be familiar with. Photographs alongside the minibeasts show children grouped and made up to resemble the insects featured. Smaller versions of all the photographs are repeated on pages 14 and 15. This non-fiction book is paired with a story on the same theme: *The Picnic* by Monica Hughes.

A simple information book

Early Learning Goals: Knowledge and understanding of the world: Similarity and difference; Creative development Explore colour, texture, shape, form and space; Use imagination in art and design

Pink A / Band 1A

Cars

Monica Hughes

A non-fiction book looking at a variety of car types in different colours, accompanied by simple, repetitive text which reinforces common colour words. Each car is photographed both in isolation, and then in its surroundings – on the race track, in the city or off the road. Pages 14 and 15 give children the opportunity to recap and discuss the text.

A non-fiction report

Early Learning Goals: Knowledge and understanding of the world: Find out about features of objects they observe

Learning objectives	High frequency words	Interest words	Related resources
NLS Framework Objectives YR T1d Track the text in the right order, page by page, left to right, top to bottom, pointing while reading, and making one-to-one correspondences. W2a Hearing and identifying initial sounds in words. *PiPs Playing with Sounds* Step 2 Hearing and saying phonemes in initial position. *Speaking and Listening objective* *ELG* Communication, language and literacy: Use language to imagine and recreate roles and experiences *Scottish 5–14 Strands:* Listening, Talking, Reading, Writing, Level A	the	rug, basket, drinks, cakes, sandwiches, wasps	*Big Book of Non-fiction A*: pp 20–21 links to the topic of food choice. **PCM 16**: Children complete the labels of the picnic items
NLS Framework Objectives YR T1d Track the text in the right order, page by page, left to right, top to bottom; T2 Use a variety of cues when reading, and aware of making sense grammatically. *Early Learning Goals:* Communication, language and literacy: Know that print carries meaning; and reads left to right, top to bottom; Understand that information can be found in non-fiction texts. *Scottish 5–14 Strands:* Listening, Talking, Reading, Writing, Level A	a	minibeasts, snail, spider, worm, caterpillar, butterfly, ladybird	*Big Book of Non-fiction B*: pp 16–17 'A Year in Aidan's Garden' links to the theme of minibeasts. **PCM 17**: Children are asked to write initial letters in the labels for the minibeasts illustrated.
NLS Framework Objectives YR T1a To recognise printed words in a variety of settings, e.g. labels, captions; W11 To make collections of words linked to particular topics. *Early Learning Goal* Communication, language and literacy: Extend vocabulary exploring the meanings and sounds of new words *Speaking and listening objective* *ELG* Communication, language and literacy: Use talk to organise, sequence and clarify thinking, ideas, feelings and events *Scottish 5–14 Strands:* Listening, Talking, Reading, Writing, Level A	a	car(s), yellow, green, black, blue, red, white	*Big Book of Rhymes A*: pp5, 16–17 'Can You Find the Tiger?' and 'Ten Tubby Teddies' support work on colour words. **PCM 18**: Children colour the different cars according to their labels.

Book band	About the book	Text type	Curriculum links

Pink A / Band 1A

Pushing and Pulling

Monica Hughes and Mark Coote

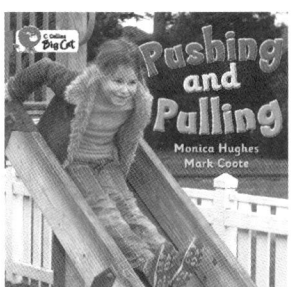

This simple non-fiction recount demonstrates different types of pushing and pulling, through photographs taken at a children's playground and simple, repetitive captions. The photographs are repeated on pages 14 and 15 under the headings 'pushing' and 'pulling'.

A simple non-fiction recount

Early Learning Goals: Physical development: Move with control and coordination

---

Pink / Band A

My Skateboard

Maoliosa Kelly and Steve Lumb

A non-fiction picture book about skateboarding. The photographs and text combine to give an account of a child getting ready and then going skateboarding. The book presents a glimpse of what it is that makes this exhilarating activity so popular. Children can recap the text with the pictorial summary of the book on pages 14 and 15.

Non-fiction recount

Early Learning Goals: Physical development: Move with control and co-ordination; Personal, Social and Emotional Development: Be confident to try new activities; respond to experiences, showing a range of feelings when appropriate

---

Pink A / Band 1A

The Guinea Pigs

Paul Shipton and Trevor Dunton

A humorous story about two guinea pigs that stray from their cage to a park before returning home again in time for breakfast. Their night-time adventure is told through a series of illustrations with very simple, repetitive text. A storyboard on pages 14 and 15 shows the sequence of events at a glance.

A story with a predictable structure and patterned language

Early Learning Goals: Knowledge and Understanding of the World; Citizenship: Animals and us

Learning objectives	High frequency words	Interest words	Related resources
NLS Framework Objectives YR T2 Use a variety of cues when reading, knowledge of the story and its context, and awareness of making grammatical sense; T3 Re-read a text to provide context cues to help read unfamiliar words; T8 Locate and read significant parts of the text, e.g. picture captions. *Speaking and listening objective* *ELG* Communication, language and literacy: interact with others, negotiating plans and activities and taking turns in conversation *Scottish 5–14 Strands:* Listening, Talking, Reading, Writing, Level A	I, am	pushing, pulling	*Big Book of Non-fiction A*: pp20–21 'What did you do at school today?' supports further work on action words. **PCM 19** gives children the opportunity to identify more 'pushing' and 'pulling'.
NLS Framework Objectives YR T7: Using knowledge of familiar texts to re-enact or re-tell to others, recounting the main points in correct sequence; W2a: Hearing and identifying initial sounds in words. *PiPs Playing with Sounds* Step 2: hear and say phonemes in initial position: *s*, *m*, *h* *Scottish 5–14 Strands:* Listening, Talking, Reading, Writing, Level A	my	pads, skateboard, helmet, friends, turn	*Big Book of Non-fiction A*: pp2–7 'My School' can be used to support work on non-fiction recounts, and on words with initial phonemes *s*, *m* and *h*. **PCM 20**: Children complete the labels on the skateboarder. **CD-ROM A**: *My Skateboard* is a Talking Book. It includes three related activities and an opportunity for free writing.
Primary Framework objectives Foundation Stage Understanding and interpreting texts: Re-tell narratives in the correct sequence, drawing on the language patterns of stories; Know that print carries meaning and, in English, is read from left to right and top to bottom. Engaging with and responding to texts: Show an understanding of the elements of stories, such as main character, sequence of events, and openings. *Primary Framework objectives Year 1* Drama: Explore familiar themes and characters through improvisation and role-play. *Scottish 5–14 Strands:* Listening, Talking, Reading, Writing, Level A	in, the	cage, garden, car, park	Simple sentences from the book are repeated on **PCM 21** for children to complete using the key words: cage, garden, car, park.

Book band	About the book	Text type	Curriculum links

Pink A / Band 1A

Shapes

Monica Hughes

A simple non-fiction book that introduces the shapes: square, triangle, circle, rectangle, star and hexagon. Each labelled shape is accompanied by a photograph showing the shape in an environmental context. For example, a rectangular brick in a wall; a hexagon in a honeycomb. All six shapes and photographs are repeated on pages 14 and 15.

A simple non-fiction book

Early Learning Goals: Mathematical Development: Use language to describe the shape and size of solid and flat shapes; Numeracy: Shape and Space – 2-D and 3-D shapes; Art & Design: Mother Nature, designer

---

Pink A / Band 1A

In the Boat

Paul Shipton and Trevor Dunton

A humorous story about a mouse with a boat taxi that picks up an increasing number of animals as it floats downstream, before eventually sinking and ending up on the riverbed! Simple text counts the number of each type of animal, from one to six, as they enter the boat. The labelled flow diagram on pages 14 and 15 retells the story and allows children to count the animals again.

A patterned story with predictable structure

Early Learning Goals: Mathematical Development: Say and use numbers; Count up to ten everyday objects; Begin to relate addition to combining objects, and subtraction to 'taking away'. Knowledge and Understanding of the World: Ask questions about why things happen

---

Pink A / Band 1A

How Many Animals?

Lee Newman and Antony Elworthy

This non-fiction counting book shows photographs of the following animals: one crocodile, two elephants, three lions, four birds, five frogs and six rabbits. Pictures of equal numbers of children add an element of fun to the book as they pretend to be the animals. The photographs of the animals and children repeated in numerical order on pages 14 and 15 encourage children to count the animals again.

A simple information book

Early Learning Goals: Mathematical Development: Counting and adding. Knowledge and Understanding of the World: Identify features of living things

Learning objectives	High frequency words	Interest words	Related resources
Primary Framework objectives Foundation Stage Understanding and interpreting texts: Show an understanding of the elements of stories, such as main character, sequence of events, and openings. Word recognition: Read some high frequency words; Hear and say sounds in words in the order in which they occur. *Primary Framework objectives Year 1* Group discussion and interaction: Ask and answer questions, make relevant contributions, offer suggestions and take turns. *Scottish 5–14 Strands:* Listening, Talking, Reading, Writing, Level A	a	square, triangle, circle, rectangle, star, hexagon, shapes	**PCM 22** features a house with several shapes incorporated into it. Children can identify the shapes and join them to the corresponding labels.
Primary Framework objectives Foundation Stage Speaking/Group discussion and interaction: Use talk to organise, sequence and clarify thinking, ideas, feelings and events. Listening and Responding: Listen with enjoyment and respond to stories. Word recognition: Read simple words by sounding out and blending the phonemes; Read some high frequency words (numbers); Read a range of familiar and common words and simple sentences independently. Understanding and interpreting texts: Show an understanding of the elements of stories, such as main character, sequence of events. *Scottish 5–14 Strands:* Listening, Talking, Reading, Writing, Level A	one, two, three, four, five, six, in, is, the, who	one, two, three, four, five, mouse, rabbits, cats, dogs, elephants, fish, taxi	**PCM 23**: Children write labels under pictures of the increasing numbers of animals that ride in the boat.
Primary Framework objectives Foundation Stage Speaking/Group discussion and interaction: Use talk to organise, sequence and clarify thinking ideas, feelings and events. Listening and Responding: Extend their vocabulary, exploring the meanings and sounds of new words; Sustain attentive listening, responding to what they have heard by relevant comments, questions or actions. Word recognition: Read some high frequency words (numbers); Hear and say sounds in words in the order in which they occur. *Scottish 5–14 Strands:* Listening, Talking, Reading, Writing, Level A	one, two, three, four, five, six	one, two, three, four, five, six, rabbits, frogs, birds, lions, elephants, crocodile, animals	**PCM 24**: Children match the correct numbers to pictures of the animals.

Book band	About the book	Text type	Curriculum links

The See-saw

Paul Shipton and Brett Hudson

A humorous story about a Hippo who wants to have a go on a see-saw. But no other animal is heavy enough to get Hippo off the ground. It takes a group of animals to do it – and in the end, it is a tiny mouse that makes the difference! Pages 14 and 15 feature a flow chart, retelling the story in sequence.

A story with a predictable structure and patterned language

Early Learning Goals: Knowledge and understanding of the world: Why things happen and how things work; Mathematical Development: using words like 'heavier/lighter' to compare quantities

Pink B / Band 1B

The Big Splash

Maureen Haselhurst and Nick Schon

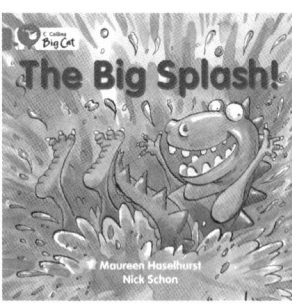

A humorous picture story, with simple, repetitive text, about a dinosaur preparing to take a dip. She gathers together all the things she needs: her boat, her shark, her armbands, her flippers, her goggles. Once everything is to hand, she is ready... to take a bath! A labelled illustration on pages 14 and 15 shows the dinosaur happily splashing around in her bath with all her swimming paraphernalia around her.

A story with predictable structure and patterned language

Early Learning Goals: Personal social and emotional development: Dress and undress independently and manage their own hygiene; Knowledge and understanding of the world: Ask questions about why things happen

Pink B / Band 1B

The Robot

Paul Shipton and Gary Dunn

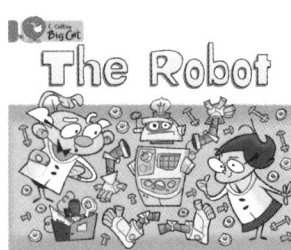

A humorous story about making a robot, naming each body part as it is added: *leg, foot, arm, hand, head*. As the different parts are used, a repeated reply of *thank you* reinforces the phrase. The body parts are repeated in a single, labelled diagram of the completed robot on pages 14 and 15.

A patterned story with predictable structure

Early Learning Goals: Knowledge and understanding of the world: Build and construct with a wide range of objects

Pink B / Band 1B

Learning objectives	High frequency words	Interest words	Related resources
NLS Framework Objectives YR T9 Be aware of story structures e.g. actions and reactions, consequences and build up and conclusion. *PiPs Playing with Sounds* Step 2: Hear and say phonemes in initial position *Early Learning Goal* Communication, language and literacy: Show an understanding of the elements of stories. *Scottish 5–14 Strands:* Listening, Talking, Reading, Writing, Level A	up, went, the, and, down	see-saw, monkey, crocodile, lion, mouse, hippo, animals	*Big Book of Rhymes A*: p4 'Hippo! Hippo!' by John Foster links with the same theme and characters. **PCM 25**: Children draw two more animal characters and episodes of the story.
NLS Framework Objectives YR T7: Use knowledge of familiar texts to re-tell main points in the correct sequence; T9: Drawing on language patterns in stories, sustain attentive listening; S3: That words are ordered left to right and need to be read that way; W2e: Hear and say initial and final sounds in words. *Early Learning Goals* Communication, language and literacy: Know that print carries meaning and is read from left to right and top to bottom. *Speaking and listening objective* ELG Communication, language and literacy: Retell narratives in the correct sequence, drawing on language patterns of stories *Scottish 5–14 Strands:* Listening, Talking, Reading, Writing, Level A	she, is, get (getting), big, the	shark, armbands, flippers, goggles, boat, bath	*Big Book of Rhymes A*: p6 'Splash!' links to the same theme and supports further work on initial and final sounds. **PCM 26**: Children add labels to the artwork.
NLS Framework Objectives YR T1d: Track the text in the right order, page by page, left to right, top to bottom; pointing while reading and one-to-one matching; T3: Re-read text to provide context cues to read unfamiliar words W5: Read on sight a range of familiar words *Speaking, Listening, Learning teaching objectives* *ELG:* Communication, language and literacy: Speak clearly and audibly and use conventions like 'please' and 'thank you' *Scottish 5–14 Strands:* Listening, Talking, Reading, Writing, Level A	here, is, a, an, where, the	head, arm, hand, leg, foot, body, thanks	*Big Book of Rhymes A*: pp 2–3 'Shake Your Leg', by John Foster, introduces different parts of the body. **PCM 27**: Children can write labels for the robot's different body parts. **CD-ROM A**: *The Robot* is a Talking Book. It includes three related activities and an opportunity for free writing.

Book band	About the book	Text type	Curriculum links

Pink B / Band 1B

Fly Away Home

Shoo Rayner

A patterned and predictable animal story about a ladybird looking for a home. She is rebuffed by other animals, until finally she finds an unusual place that makes her happy. The story map on pages 14 and 15 shows the route Ladybird took, and allows children to recap the story. Shoo Rayner also wrote and illustrated the Lilac story *Cat and Dog*.

A patterned story with predictable structure

Early Learning Goals: Knowledge and understanding of the world: Look closely at similarities, differences, patterns and change; Creative development: Explore colour, texture, shape, form

---

Pink B / Band 1B

The Pond

Claire Llewellyn and Martin Sanders

A non-fiction report about the various creatures in a typical pond: frog, snails, dragonflies, pond-skaters, fish, bird. All of these are repeated in a single, labelled diagram on pages 14 and 15. This information book is paired with a story on the same theme: *Fly Away Home* by Shoo Rayner.

A simple non-fiction report

Early Learning Goals: Knowledge and understanding of the world: find out about features of living things; observe features of the natural world; find out about their environment

---

Pink B / Band 1B

Wheels

Frances Ridley

This non-fiction picture book takes a look at all sorts of wheels through a series of labelled photographs: big and small, fat and thin, fast and slow. The wheels are photographed from different angles. A chart on pages 14 and 15 reproduces the photographs of wheels side by side as opposite pairs.

A simple non-fiction text

Early Learning Goals: Knowledge and understanding of the world: Look closely at similarities, differences, patterns and change

Learning objectives	High frequency words	Interest words	Related resources
NLS Framework Objectives YR T1d: Track the text in the right order, page by page, left to right, top to bottom; pointing while reading and one-to-one matching. T2: Use a variety of cues when reading: knowledge of the story and its context, and awareness of how it should make sense grammatically. *PiPs Playing with Sounds* Step 2: Hear and say phonemes in initial position *Speaking, Listening, Learning objective Y1* T1 Discussion 3: Ask and answer questions, make relevant contributions. *Scottish 5–14 Strands:* Listening, Talking, Reading, Writing, Level A	is, on, the, away, at	ladybird, fly, away, tree, ground, earth, shed, pond, flower, home, last	*Big Book of Rhymes A*: pp 2–3 'Shake Your Leg' supports work on initial sounds *sh* and *fl*. **PCM 28**: Children complete the missing initial sounds in the key words in a flow chart of the story.
NLS Framework Objectives YR T1d: Track the text in the right order, page by page, left to right, top to bottom, pointing while reading; W6: Read on sight NLS high frequency words; T1a: Recognise printed words in a variety of settings, e.g. labels. *Speaking and Listening objective* *ELG:* Communication, Language and Literacy: Use talk to organise ideas *Scottish 5–14 Strands:* Listening, Talking, Reading, Writing, Level A	can, see, we, a	pond, bird, frogs, fish, snails, dragonflies, pond-skaters	**PCM 29**: Provides a chart for children to record their findings on a nature trek.
NLS Framework Objectives YR T2 Use a variety of cues when reading: text patterning, knowledge of story, context and grammatical sense; T8 Locate and read significant parts of the text, e.g. labels; S2 Use awareness of grammar of a sentence and repeated patterns to make predictions and check reading. *Early Learning Goal* Communication, Language and Literacy: Extend vocabulary, exploring the meaning and sounds of new words. *Speaking and Listening objective* *ELG* Communication, language and literacy: Use talk to organise and clarify thinking, ideas, feelings and events *Scottish 5–14 Strands:* Listening, Talking, Reading, Writing, Level A	and, are	big, wheels, small, fat, thin, fast, slow	**PCM 30**: Children write labels to accompany the pictures of wheels.

Book band	About the book	Text type	Curriculum links

Pink B / Band 1B

Come to the Circus!

Damian Harvey and Sally Denton

A non-fiction book about circus performers including the clowns, the dancers, the juggler and the acrobats. A combination of illustrations and photographs show them at work. A poster on pages 14 and 15 advertises when and where the circus can be seen, and is ideal for children to discuss and recap the text.

A simple information book

Early Learning Goals: Knowledge and understanding of the world: Find out some features of events, objects and living things

Cats

Claire Llewellyn and Andrew Beckett

This simple non-fiction book compares pet cats and wild cats, pointing out the features common to both through labelled illustrations and photographs. All the labels are repeated in a single diagram on pages 14 and 15: *eyes*, *ears*, *teeth*, *fur*, *legs*, *tail*.

A non-fiction report

Early Learning Goals: Knowledge and understanding of the world: Find out about and identify some features of living things; look closely at similarities, differences, patterns and change

Colour Bears

Tasha Pym and Liz Pichon

Colour Bears introduces the principles of colour-mixing through a simple story about polar bears having fun with paint. The bears' snowy white world is soon splattered with colour as they experiment with different paint effects. The text includes seven colour words. A diagram on pages 14 and 15 summarises the colour-mixing information pictorially.

A story with a predictable structure and patterned language

Early Learning Goals: Creative Development: Explore what happens when you mix colour; Mathematical Development: Use developing mathematical ideas to solve problems

Learning objectives	High frequency words	Interest words	Related resources
NLS Framework Objectives YR S2: Use awareness of grammar of sentences, language patterns and the meaning of the text to predict words. W5, W7: Read on sight a range of familiar words and words of appropriate difficulty. *Speaking and listening objectives* ELG Communication, language and literacy: Interact with others, negotiating and taking turns; use language to imagine and recreate roles and experiences *Scottish 5–14 Strands:* Listening, Talking, Reading, Writing, Level A	come, and, see, the	circus, clowns, dancers, juggler, magician, acrobats, tightrope walker	**PCM 31**: A template for designing a poster advertising a circus.
NLS Framework Objectives YR T1a: Recognise printed words in a variety of settings, e.g. labels; T1d: Point while reading and making one-to-one correspondence between spoken and written words; W11: Make collections of words linked to particular topics *Speaking and Listening objective* ELG Communication, language and literacy: Use talk to organise and clarify feelings and ideas *Scottish 5–14 Strands:* Listening, Talking, Reading, Writing, Level A	a, cat	has, eyes, ears, teeth, fur, legs, tail	*Big Book of Rhymes A*: pp 5 and 22–23 'Can You Find the Tiger?' and 'The MOQ Cat' by Jan Pollard support work on the theme of cats. **PCM 32**: Children join the labels to the correct part of the cat diagram. **CD-ROM A**: *Cats* is a Talking Book. It includes three related activities and an opportunity for free writing.
Primary Framework objectives Foundation Stage Engaging with and responding to texts: Know that print carries meaning and, in English, is read from left to right and top to bottom. Understanding and interpreting texts: Extend their vocabulary, exploring the meaning and sounds of new words. *Primary Framework objectives Year 1* Group discussion and interaction: Ask and answer questions, make relevant contributions, offer suggestions and take turns. *Scottish 5–14 Strands:* Listening, Talking, Reading, Writing, Level A	and, make, do	colour, bears, red, blue, purple, yellow, orange, green, brown	**PCM 33** provides further practice in recognising colour words.

Book band	About the book		Text type	Curriculum links

Pink B / Band 1B

We Like Fruit

Gill Budgell and Steve Lumb

This non-fiction text is a report on the fruits that a group of children enjoy eating. Labelled photographs, showing each fruit growing in its natural environment, are accompanied by the simple caption: 'I like eating…'. All six fruits are shown in a labelled diagram on pages 14 and 15.

A non-fiction report

Early Learning Goals: Knowledge and Understanding of the World; Mathematical Development; Creative Development

Pink B / Band 1B

Monster Mess

Tasha Pym and Olivia Villet

A humorous story with simple, repetitive text about two little monsters painting spots, stripes, squares, zigzags and triangles. But what are they painting? Finally, the reader discovers the little monsters have actually been painting the shapes on their sleeping mum! Pages 14 and 15 feature the fully painted mum-monster, with smaller pictures of the little monsters from the story to remind children of the shapes they painted. Leader lines connect these pictures to show where these shapes are painted on to mum-monster's body.

A story with a predictable structure and patterned language

Early Learning Goals: Creative Development: Explore colour and shape. Mathematical Development: Recognise and recreate simple patterns and shapes. Knowledge and Understanding of the World: Look closely at similarities, differences, patterns

Pink B / Band 1B

I Can Do It!

Paul Shipton and Antony Elworthy

A simple information book depicting different activities: running, jumping, hanging, skating, creeping and swimming. Simple text accompanies photographs of animals performing each activity, alongside photographs of children acting out the same activity. The photographs are repeated on pages 14 and 15 with a one-word label to describe the activity.

A simple information book

Early Learning Goals: Communication, Language and Literacy: Use language to imagine and recreate roles and experiences. Knowledge of the World: Identify some features of living things. Physical Development: Move with confidence, imagination and in safety

Learning objectives	High frequency words	Interest words	Related resources
Primary Framework objectives Foundation Stage Understanding and interpreting texts: Extend their vocabulary, exploring the meaning and sounds of new words; Show an understanding of the elements of stories, such as main character, sequence of events, and openings, and how information can be found in non-fiction texts to answer questions about where, who, why and how. Group discussion and interaction: Interact with others, negotiating plans and activities and taking turns in conversation *Scottish 5 14 Strands:* Listening, Talking, Reading, Writing, Level A	I, like, we, all	fruit, label, apples, bananas, grapes, oranges, melons, strawberries	**PCM 34** provides a table for children to record which fruits they and their friends like eating.
Primary Framework objectives Foundation Stage Sentence structure and punctuation: Write their own names and other things such as labels and captions. Speaking/Listening and responding: Extend their vocabulary, exploring the meanings and sounds of new words. Listening and responding: Sustain attentive listening, responding to what they have heard by relevant comments, questions or actions. Word recognition: Hear and say sounds in words in the order in which they occur; Read a range of familiar and common words and simple sentences independently. *Scottish 5–14 Strands:* Listening, Talking, Reading, Writing, Level A	are, but, like, little, mum, they to, we, what	monsters, painted, spots, stripes, squares, zigzags, triangles	**PCM 35**: Children label the shapes painted on mum-monster.
Primary Framework objectives Foundation Stage Sentence structure and punctuation: Begin to form simple sentences, sometimes using punctuation. Speaking: Use language to imagine and recreate roles and experiences. Speaking/Drama: Extend vocabulary, exploring the meaning and sounds of new words. Understanding and interpreting texts: Know that print carries meaning and, in English, is read from left to right and top to bottom. Listening and responding: Sustain attentive listening, responding to what they have heard by relevant comments, questions or actions. Word recognition: Recognise common diagraphs. *Scottish 5-14 Strands:* Listening, Talking, Reading, Writing, Level A	I, can, it, up, on	running, jumping, hanging, skating, creeping, swimming	**PCM 36**: Children fill in the missing letters for each activity and name their favourite activity.

Book band	About the book	Text type	Curriculum links

A Day Out

Claire Llewellyn and Andy Hammond

Bill's walk in the country takes him over a river, up a hill, into a wood and behind a waterfall. A few steps behind Bill, however, a hungry bear with an eye on Bill's sandwiches is not so lucky. The bear's attempts to grab the sandwiches from Bill's backpack are foiled by a variety of minor disasters. Back at the car park, Bill is not all that hungry and leaves his sandwiches, so the bear is finally rewarded. Children can follow and discuss the route taken by Bill and the bear using the map on pages 14 and 15.

A story with a predictable structure and patterned language

Early Learning Goals: Knowledge and understanding of the world: Observe, find out about and identify features in the natural world

Red A / Band 2A

Tec and the Cake

Tony Mitton and Martin Chatterton

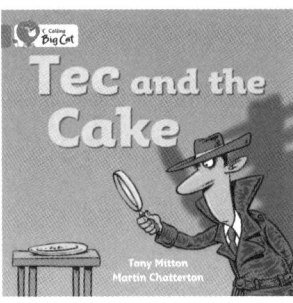

A detective story, by a significant author, in which Tec sets out to discover who has eaten the missing cake. Using a spy glass, Tec follows a trail of crumbs, passing a number of indignant-looking pets along the way. The trail finally leads him to a basket belonging to the guilty dog. A gameboard on pages 14 and 15 shows the trail of crumbs that Tec followed leading him from the cake to the dog; children can make up their own rules for playing the game. *Tec and the Cake* is one of three stories by Tony Mitton about Tec the Detective.

A story with a predictable structure and patterned language

Early Learning Goals: Personal, social and emotional development: Understanding what is right and wrong and why

Red A / Band 2A

Tec and the Hole

Tony Mitton and Martin Chatterton

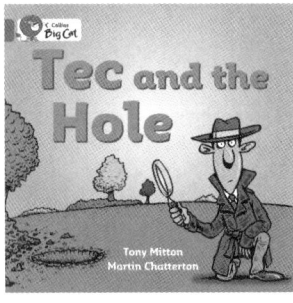

A detective story, by a significant author, in which Tec sets out to discover who dug the hole in the lawn. Tec's investigation involves many suspects, all of whom can be seen in a character line-up on pages 14 and 15. *Tec and the Hole* is one of three stories by Tony Mitton about Tec the Detective.

A story with predictable structure and patterned language

Early Learning Goals: Personal, social and emotional development: Understanding what is right and wrong and why

Red A / Band 2A

Learning objectives	High frequency words	Interest words	Related resources
NLS Framework Objectives YR T1d Track the text in the right order, page by page, left to right, top to bottom, pointing while reading, and one-to-one matching; T7 Use knowledge of texts to recount the main points of the story in sequence; W2a Hearing and identifying initial sounds in words. *PiPs Playing with Sounds* Step 2: Hearing and saying phonemes in initial position. *Speaking and Listening objective* *ELG* Communication, language and literacy: Use language to imagine and recreate roles and experiences. *Scottish 5–14 Strands:* Listening, Talking, Reading, Writing, Level A	a, for, he, went, to, up	over, up, behind, into	**PCM 37**: Children recall and write events of the story in the correct sequence.
NLS Framework Objectives YR T1d Track the text in the right order, page by page, left to right, top to bottom, pointing while reading, and one-to-one matching; S1 Expect written text to make sense and check for sense if it does not; W6 Read on sight the 45 high frequency words to be taught by the end of YR. *PiPs Playing with Sounds* Steps 2 and 3: Know phoneme-grapheme correspondences: s c, t, h, d, sh. *Speaking, Listening and Learning objectives* Y1 T2 Speaking: Retell stories, ordering events using story language. *Scottish 5–14 Strands:* Listening, Talking, Reading, Writing, Level A	the, was, it, cat, dog	who, ate, cake, hamster, fish	**PCM 38**: Children put the story into sequence.
NLS Framework Objectives YR T1c Understand and use correctly terms about books and print: book, cover, beginning, end, page, line, word, letter, title; T1d Track the text in the right order, page by page, left to right, top to bottom, pointing while reading, and making one-to-one correspondences T2 Use a variety of cues when reading: knowledge of the story and its context, and awareness of grammatical sense. *Speaking and listening objective* ELG Communication, language and literacy: Retell narratives in the correct sequence, drawing on language patterns of stories *Scottish 5–14 Strands:* Listening, Talking, Reading, Writing, Level A	was, it, the, no, dog	who, hole, rabbit, squirrel, girl, man	**PCM 39**: Children design a new cover for *Tec and the Hole*. **CD-ROM A**: *Tec and the Hole* is a Talking Book. It includes three related activities and an opportunity for free writing.

Book band	About the book	Text type	Curriculum links

Red A / Band 2A

The Beach

Alison Hawes and Lisa Smith

A patterned picture story about a family outing to the beach. The high-frequency words, *'Look! We can see…'* are repeated throughout the story as the children spot *seagulls*, *an ice-cream van*, *sand*, *the sea*, *Mum and Dad*, and *the beach* from the back seat of the car. Pages 14 and 15 show a labelled beach scene, incorporating the key words from the text. This story is paired with a non-fiction book on the same theme: *Shapes on the Seashore* by Frances Ridley.

A story with predictable structure and patterned language

Early Learning Goals: Knowledge and understanding of the world: Look closely at similarity and differences; Observe and find out about features in the natural world

---

Red A / Band 2A

Shapes on the Seashore

Frances Ridley and Ali Teo

Shapes on the Seashore is a non-fiction recount of a boy and his mother exploring the shapes of various creatures and items they find on the seashore. They later use several of the things they find to decorate a sandcastle. The shapes are repeated on pages 14 and 15 for children to recall and discuss.

A simple recount

Early Learning Goals: Knowledge and understanding of the world: Find out about, and identify, some features of living things, objects and events they observe

---

Red A / Band 2A

What's Inside?

Monica Hughes

A non-fiction picture book that takes a close-up look at what can be found inside a pod, nutshell, pupa, hive and egg, as well as what's inside you and me. Pages 14 and 15 provides an opportunity for children to recap and discuss the text.

A simple information book

Early Learning Goals: Knowledge and understanding of the world: Find out about, and identify, some features of living things, objects and events they observe

Learning objectives	High frequency words	Interest words	Related resources
NLS Framework Objectives YR T1d Track the text in the right order, page by page, left to right, top to bottom, pointing while reading, and one-to-one matching; T2 Use a variety of cues when reading; including knowledge of the story; W2 Identifying initial sounds in words. *Speaking, Listening, Learning objective Y1* T1 Listening 2: Listen with sustained concentration *Scottish 5–14 Strands:* Listening, Talking, Reading, Writing, Level A	look, I, can, see, the, mum, and, dad	seagulls, ice-cream van, sand, sea, beach, children	**PCM 40**: Children draw or label the things that the children in the story saw on their car journey to the beach.
NLS Framework Objectives YR S2 Use awareness of the grammar of a sentence to make predictions W2b Read letters that represent the sound 'sh'; W11 Make collections of words linked to particular topics, i.e. shape and shore. *Speaking and Listening objective* ELG Communication, language and literacy: Interact with others, negotiating and taking turns. *Scottish 5–14 Strands:* Listening, Talking, Reading, Writing, Level A	we, a, you	seashore, star, starfish, circle, jellyfish, oval, pebble, rectangle, razor shell, spiral	**PCM 41**: Children draw and label objects which have particular shapes.
NLS Framework Objectives YR T1c Understand and use correctly terms about books and print (e.g. cover, title, label); W2 Read letters that represent sounds, e.g. b, p, s, w; W5 Read on sight a range of familiar words, e.g. labels; W11 Make collections of words linked to particular topics. *Speaking and Listening objective* ELG Communication, language and literacy: Use talk to organise, sequence and clarify thinking. *Scottish 5–14 Strands:* Listening, Talking, Reading, Writing, Level A	is, in, this, you, and, me	pod, inside, pea, nut, walnut, pupa, butterfly, hive, bees, egg, snake (or turtle), skeleton	*Big Book of Rhymes A*: pp 8–9 'Caterpillar, Caterpillar' links to the theme of nature and 'what's inside?' **PCM 42**: Children make labelled drawings showing what's inside other things.

Book band	About the book	Text type	Curriculum links

Red A / Band 2A

In the Dark

Claire Llewellyn and Karen Oppatt

A patterned non-fiction text coupled with atmospheric illustrations to show what happens in the neighbourhood when it is dark. Who can be found in the city streets when children are tucked up in bed? Which animals prowl in the wood by the light of the moon? Pages 14 and 15 repeat the scenes explored throughout the book, allowing children the chance to recap on the narrative, and answer the question 'Where is it dark?'

Non-fiction recount

Early Learning Goals: Knowledge and understanding of the world: features of the events they observe; features of the natural world; asking questions about why things happen

Red A / Band 2A

Up, Up and Away

Sue Graves

A non-fiction recount about the journey of a child's red balloon that flies over several interesting landscapes including rooftops, a river, a mountain and the sea. The flow chart on pages 14 and 15 allows children to discuss and recap the balloon's journey.

A simple non-fiction recount

Early Learning Goals: Knowledge and understanding of the world: Observe, find out about and identify features in the place they live and the natural world

Red A / Band 2A

Cat and Dog Play Hide and Seek

Shoo Rayner

A comical story, by a significant author, told through a series of pictures and questions. Where is Cat? Dog is looking in all the wrong places: under the table, behind the chair, under the bed and in the cupboard. Finally, Cat's whereabouts become apparent when Dog switches on a light and Cat comes crashing down from the light shade. A story map on pages 14 and 15 illustrates an aerial view of the route that Dog took when searching for Cat.

A story with a predictable structure and patterned language

Early Learning Goals: Personal, Social and Emotional Development: Work as part of a group, taking turns and sharing fairly

Learning objectives	High frequency words	Interest words	Related resources
NLS Framework Objectives YR T1C: Understand and use correctly terms about books and print… W2A: Hear and identify initial sounds in words *Progression in Phonics* Step 2 Hear and say phonemes in initial position. *Speaking and Listening objective* ELG Communication, language and literacy: Use talk to organise, sequence and clarify thinking, ideas feeling and events *Scottish 5–14 Strands:* Listening, Talking, Reading, Writing, Level A	it, is, in, the	dark, park, street, city, wood, home	*Big Book of Rhymes A*: p7 'Girls and Boys' shares the theme of night time and can support work on initial sounds. **PCM 43**: Children fill in the initial sounds and then write and draw another night scene. **CD-Rom A**: *In the Dark* is a Talking Book. It includes three related activities and an opportunity for free writing, with a bank of useful words and punctuation.
NLS Framework Objectives YR T1c Understanding and using terms about books and print: cover, illustration, word, letter, title; T1d To track the text in the right order, page by page, left to right, top to bottom, pointing while reading, and making one-to-one correspondences; W2a Hear and say initial phonemes in words. *Speaking, listening and learning objective Y1* T1 Group discussion 3: Ask and answer questions, offer suggestions and take turns. *Scottish 5–14 Strands:* Listening, Talking, Reading, Writing, Level A	the, up, and, away, it	goes, over, balloon, house, town, river, mountain, sea	**PCM 44**: A writing frame for children to recount the balloon's journey.
Primary Framework objectives Foundation Stage Engaging with and responding to texts: Know that print carries meaning and, in English, is read from left to right and top to bottom. Understanding and interpreting texts: Re-tell narratives in the correct sequence, drawing on the language patterns of stories. Word recognition: Read some high frequency words; Hear and say sounds in words in the order in which they occur. Listening and responding: Sustain attentive listening, responding to what they have heard by relevant comments, questions or actions. *Scottish 5–14 Strands:* Listening, Talking, Reading, Writing, Level A	cat, and, dog, is, he, the, in	where, under, table, behind, chair, bed, cupboard, oops	**PCM 45** asks a series of questions about Cat's whereabouts for children to answer *yes* or *no* to.

Book band	About the book	Text type	Curriculum links

Red A / Band 2A

My Bike Ride

Maoliosa Kelly and Ley Honor Roberts

A simple non-fiction text about a bicycle journey. The text and pictures recount the different stages of a journey from the start to the end. There are several road signs to spot along the way, in addition to different landscape features and other forms of transport such as a train, an aeroplane and a hot air balloon. A map on pages 14 and 15 enables the reader to retrace the journey.

A simple non-fiction recount

Early Learning Goals: Geography: Where in the World is Barnaby Bear?; Investigating our local area

Red A / Band 2A

Have You Ever?

Tasha Pym and Antony Elworthy

A fun story that follows a boy through a fantastical land of weird and wonderful creatures. Imaginative illustrations complement the text, which invites children to envisage using each of their five senses, by asking if they have you ever seen, heard, touched, smelt, or tasted any of these creatures. A story map on pages 14 and 15 lets the children recap and discuss the story.

A story with a predictable structure and patterned language

Early Learning Goals: Creative Development: Explore colour, texture, shape, form and space in two and three dimensions; Respond in a variety of ways to what they see, hear, smell, touch and taste

Red A / Band 2A

Weather Report

Alison Hawes and Manya Stojic

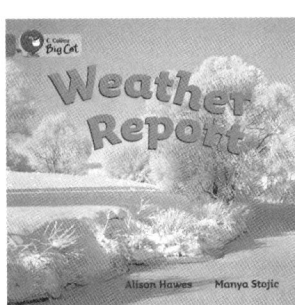

A non-fiction report about different types of weather over the course of a week. Photographs of each type of weather accompany illustrations of how people might act and dress in different weather conditions, while the repetitive pattern of the text reports on each day's weather. A summary "Weather Report" on pages 14 and 15, provides children with the opportunity to recap on the different weather-types and the days of the week.

A non-fiction report

Early Learning Goals: Knowledge and Understanding of the World: Find out about and identify some features of events they observe. Creative Development: Respond in a variety of ways to what they see, hear, smell, touch and feel

Learning objectives	High frequency words	Interest words	Related resources
Primary Framework objectives Foundation Stage Engaging with and responding to texts: Show an understanding of the elements of stories, such as main character, sequence of events, and openings. Understanding and interpreting texts: Re-tell narratives in the correct sequence, drawing on the language patterns of stories. Word recognition: Read some high frequency words; Read simple words by sounding out and blending the phonemes all through the word from left to right. *Primary Framework objectives Year 1* Speaking: Tell stories and describe incidents from their own experience in an audible voice. *Scottish 5–14 Strands:* Listening, Talking, Reading, Writing, Level A	on, my, up, the, going	getting, bike, up, hill, down, turn, right, left, off, map	**PCM 46** shows a map like the one on pages 14 and 15. Children may need to re-read the book to remind themselves of the different geographical features they need to draw on the map.
Primary Framework objectives Foundation Stage Sentence structure and punctuation: Write their own names and other things such as labels and captions and begin to form simple sentences, sometimes using punctuation. Speaking/Responding and listening: Extend their vocabulary, exploring the meanings and sounds of new words. Understanding and interpreting texts: Know that print carries meaning and, in English, is read from left to right and top to bottom; Retell narrative in the correct sequence, drawing on the language patterns of stories. Word recognition: Recognise common diagraphs. *Scottish 5-14 Strands:* Listening, Talking, Reading, Writing, Level A	Have, you, seen	sneep, horp, tiffler, smorp, thoo	**PCM 47**: Children name which part of the body was used to meet each creature.
Primary Framework objectives Foundation Stage Speaking: Use language to imagine and recreate roles and experiences. Understanding and interpreting texts: Know that print carries meaning and, in English, is read from left to right and top to bottom. Listening and responding: Sustain attentive listening, responding to what they have heard by relevant comments, questions or actions. Word recognition: Blend letters to read words and recognise common diagraphs. *Scottish 5–14 Strands:* Listening, Talking, Reading, Writing, Level A	it, was, on, and	Monday, Tuesday, Wednesday, Thursday, Friday, Saturday, Sunday, sunny, cloudy, rainy, windy, foggy, snowy.	**PCM 48**: Children draw or write what the weather was like on each day of the week in the book. They also name the current day of the week, and describe that day's weather.

Book band	About the book	Text type	Curriculum links

Pirates

Paul Shipton and Kelly Waldek

A patterned counting text about a band of pirates searching for treasure. One-by-one, they get into trouble and make a hasty retreat back to the pirate ship. The map on pages 14 and 15 shows the trail the pirates take from their ship to the treasure cave and back again, and can be used to help recap and retell the story. Paul Shipton is also the author of *See-saw*, *Get the Fruit!* and *The Robot*.

A story with a predictable structure and patterned language

Early Learning Goals: Creative Development: Use their imagination in role play and stories; Mathematical Development: Say and use number names in order; Find one more and one less than a number from one to ten)

Red B / Band 2B

Where is the Wind?

Celia Warren and Lisa Williams

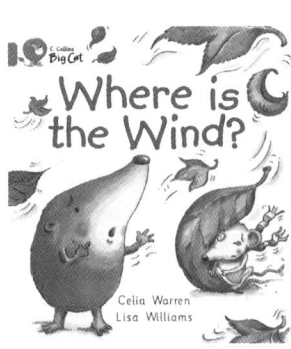

Mole sets out to see the wind. He asks every animal he meets if they see the wind and they all say no. The illustrations, however, tell a different story: windswept trees, blowing leaves and litter show that the wind is actually blowing, though invisible to them. A storyboard on pages 14 and 15 shows the trail that Mole followed.

A story with a predictable structure and patterned language

Early Learning Goals: Knowledge and understanding of the world: Find out about the features of living things, objects and events

Red B / Band 2B

Woody's Week

Michaela Morgan and Dee Shulman

A patterned and predictable story exploring the highs and lows of Woody's birthday week. An exciting present causes a big problem, but Woody cleverly solves it. Pages 14 and 15 feature a pictorial summary of Woody's week, providing opportunities to recap and to learn more about days of the week. Michaela Morgan also wrote *Rat-tat-tat* (Yellow) and *Funny Fish* (Blue).

A story with a predictable structure and patterned language

Early Learning Goals: Personal, social and emotional development: Respond to significant experiences showing a range of feelings when appropriate, form good relationships with adults and peers

Red B / Band 2B

Learning objectives	High frequency words	Interest words	Related resources
NLS Framework Objectives YR T1D: Track the text in the right order. T2: Use reading cues; knowledge/context of story, and awareness of how it should make sense grammatically. S1: Expect written text to make sense and to check for sense if it does not. S3: Understand that words are ordered left to right and need to be read that way to make sense. W6: Read on sight NLS high frequency words. *Speaking and Listening objective* ELG Communication, language and literacy: Use talk to organise, sequence and clarify thinking, ideas feeling and events *Scottish 5–14 Strands:* Listening, Talking, Reading, Writing, Level A	big, went, to, the	pirates, beach, river, trees, hill, cave, ship, number words one to five	*Big Book of Rhymes A:* pp 14–15 'Raindrops' supports work on counting words from one to ten. **PCM 49**: Children can label the treasure map with the labels supplied. **CD-Rom A**: *Pirates* is a Talking Book. It includes three related activities and an opportunity for free writing, with a bank of useful words and punctuation.
NLS Framework Objectives T1d: To track the text in the right order, page by page, left to right, top to bottom; pointing while reading, and making one-to-one correspondences; S1: To expect written text to make sense and to check for sense if it does not. *PiPs Playing with sounds* Steps 2-5: Know more phoneme-grapheme correspondences (b, s, m, g, h, t, d, l, k, w, wh, ng) *Speaking and listening objective* ELG Communication, language and literacy: Interact with others, negotiating and taking turns in conversation. *Scottish 5–14 Strands:* Listening, Talking, Reading, Writing, Level A	the, said, to, you, no, it, for	where, mole, going, see, wind, bee, hello, mouse, deer, toad, wasn't, there, looks	**PCM 50**: A writing frame to support children in rewriting the story.
NLS Framework Objectives YR T1d: Track the text in the right order, page by page, left to right, top to bottom, pointing while reading, and making one-to-one correspondence; T2: Use a variety of cues when reading; T3: Reread a text to practise context cues to help read unfamiliar words; W9: Recognise the critical features of words e.g. shape, length. *Speaking, Listening, Learning objective Y1* T2 Speaking 5 Retell stories, ordering events using story language *Scottish 5–14 Strands:* Listening, Talking, Reading, Writing, Level A	I, was, on, it, we, played, my	sad, cross, idea, happy, house, days of the week	*Big Book of Non-fiction A:* pp 10–11 'School menu' supports further work on days of the week. **PCM 51**: Children make their own diary of their week.

Book band	About the book	Text type	Curriculum links

Red B / Band 2B

Tec and the Litter

Tony Mitton and Martin Chatterton

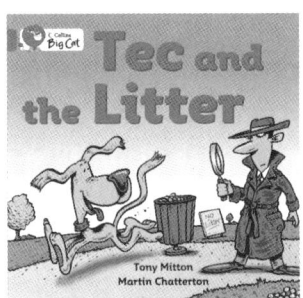

Tec the detective turns up again for another mystery. This time Tec sets out to discover who has dropped litter in the park. Tec follows the trail of litter and eventually discovers that he is the culprit, as the litter came out of a hole in his pocket! A story map on pages 14 and 15 offers children the chance to recap and discuss the story. *Tec and the Litter* is the final story of three by Tony Mitton about Tec the Detective in the *Collins Big Cat* series.

A story with predictable structure and patterned language

Early Learning Goals: Knowledge and understanding of the world: Investigate objects by using all of the senses

---

Red B / Band 2B

At the Dump

Claire Llewellyn and Ley Honor Roberts

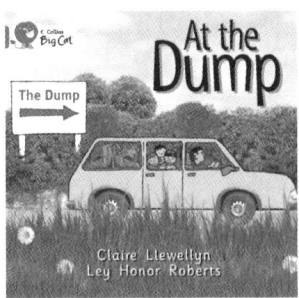

A non-fiction recount of a family trip to the dump. Simple text and labelled illustrations show how different materials are sorted into different containers at the dump ready for recycling. A diagram on pages 14 and 15 reminds the reader of the materials that were collected and the different containers they were put into at the dump. This information book is paired with a story on the same theme: *Tec and the Litter* by Tony Mitton.

A simple recount

Early Learning Goals: Knowledge and understanding of the world: Find out about their environment, and features they like and dislike

---

Red B / Band 2B

What do you like?

Anna Owen

A non-fiction recount answering the question, *What do you like to eat?* for several children over the course of a day. It features cuisines of different cultures using photographs, labels, speech bubbles and a clock face showing when different meals are typically eaten. Pages 14–15 give a pictorial summary of the book, with labelled foods arranged according to the time of day they are often eaten.

A simple non-fiction recount

Early Learning Goals: Physical development: keeping healthy and things that contribute to this

Learning objectives	High frequency words	Interest words	Related resources
NLS Framework Objectives YR T1d Track the text in the right order, page by page, left to right, top to bottom, pointing while reading, and making one-to-one correspondences T2: Use a variety of cues when reading: knowledge of the story and its context, and awareness of making sense grammatically *Early Learning Goal* Communication, Language and Literacy: Show an understanding of the elements of stories, such as main character, sequence of events *Speaking and listening objective* ELG Communication, Language and Literacy: Speak clearly and audibly with confidence, showing awareness of the listener. *Scottish 5–14 Strands:* Listening, Talking, Reading, Writing, Level A	I, can, see, a, by, the, on, in, he, said	bench, bin, can, banana, skin, packet, path, pond, bottle top, grass, hole	**PCM 52**: Children can carry out a litter survey of the school playground with this chart.
NLS Framework Objectives YR T1d: Track the text in the right order, page by page, left to right, top to bottom, pointing while reading, and making one-to-one correspondences; T2: Use a variety of cues when reading, knowledge of the story and its context, and how it should make sense grammatically; W6: Read on sight the 45 high frequency words to be taught by the end of YR. *PiPs Playing with Sounds* Steps 2-3: Reading phonemes in initial position d, g, p, h, c, t, th *Speaking, Listening and Learning objective Y1* T1 Group discussion 3 Ask and answer questions, make contributions and suggestions and take turns *Scottish 5–14 Strands:* Listening, Talking, Reading, Writing, Level A	we, went, to, the, Dad, and, it, in	dump, with, took, paper, wood, glass, cardboard, leaves, put, here, them	**PCM 53**: Children read labels in order to complete a diagram.
NLS Framework Objectives YR T1: Track the text in the right order, page by page, left to right, top to bottom, pointing while reading and one-to-one matching S2: Use awareness of grammar of sentence to predict words W5: Read on sight a range of familiar words *Speaking and Listening objectives* ELG: Sustain attentive listening, responding to what they have heard by relevant comments, questions or actions *Scottish 5–14 Strands:* Listening, Talking, Reading, Writing, Level A	I, like, you, for	breakfast, toast, snack, banana, lunch, milk, biscuit, dinner, pasta, bedtime, chocolate	*Big Book of Non-fiction A*: pp20–21 School menu links to topic of food choice. **PCM 54**: A chart for children to record their favourite foods during the course of a day.

Book band	About the book		Text type	Curriculum links

Red B / Band 2B

Let's Go Shopping

Betty Moon, Jamie Oliver and Steve Lumb

A simple non-fiction book that shows where people shop for shoes, food and other things. Photographs show children role-playing in different types of shops while illustrations show typical examples of such shops. A map on pages 14 and 15 shows the high street so children can recount the shopping trip.

A non-fiction report

Early Learning Goals: Knowledge and understanding of the world: Observe and find out about features in the place they live

Red B / Band 2B

The Oak Tree

Anna Owen and Laszlo Veres

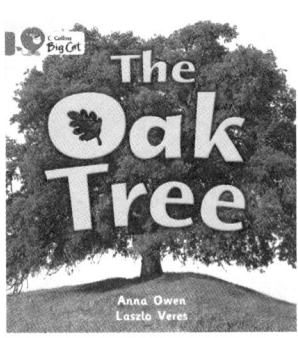

A non-fiction, photographic picture book about the different parts of an oak tree and the creatures that live in its roots, trunk, bark, branches and leaves. The photographs, including close-ups, answer the repeated question: '*Who lives…?*' There is a large, labelled diagram of an oak tree and its inhabitants on pages 14–15.

A simple non-chronological report

Early Learning Goals: Knowledge and understanding of the world: to find out about and identify some features of living things, objects and events they observe

Red B / Band 2B

What's For Breakfast?

Paul Shipton and Jon Stuart

A picture story about three hungry ants. The ants want to know what is for breakfast but they are not keen on dad's sweet offerings. Finally, he suggests an apple; an offer that everyone is happy with. The book includes several discussion features, such as speech bubbles and a clock that shows the passing of time. A story trail on pages 14 and 15 summarises the different stages of the book in sequence.

A story with a predictable structure and patterned language

Early Learning Goals: Science: Life processes and living things; Numeracy: Time; Physical Development: Keeping healthy and things that contribute to this

Learning objectives	High frequency words	Interest words	Related resources
NLS Framework Objectives YR T1a Recognise printed and handwritten words in a variety of settings, e.g. labels, signs, advertisements, newspapers; S1 Expect written text to make sense and to check for sense if it does not; W6 Read on sight high frequency words to be taught by the end of YR. *PiPs Playing with sounds* Steps 2-4: Know more phoneme-grapheme correspondences: sh, k, p, n, c, th. *Speaking, Listening, Learning objectives Y1* T1 Speaking 1 Describe incidents or tell stories from own experience, in an audible voice. *Scottish 5–14 Strands:* Listening, Talking, Reading, Writing, Level A	we, go, get, all, to, the, of, a	shoe, shop, trainers, baker's, bread, books, supermarket, sorts, things, newsagent's, comic, café, drink	**PCM 55**: Children match shops with items they buy in them.
NLS Framework Objectives YR T1a: Recognise printed and hand-written words in a variety of settings; T2, T10: Use a variety of cues when reading, including knowledge of story, sentence structure and text patterns; W11: Make collections of words linked to particular topics. *Speaking and Listening objectives* *ELG* Communication, Language and Literacy: Extend vocabulary, exploring meanings and sounds of new words. *Scottish 5–14 Strands:* Listening, Talking, Reading, Writing, Level A	this, is, a, are, the, of, in, on	roots, trunk, bark, branches, leaves, these, who, lives, oak tree, rabbit, fox, mole, woodpecker, caterpillar, butterfly, crow, wasp, beetle, ant, bat, squirrel	*Big Book of Rhymes A*: pp 8–9 and 12–13 'Caterpillar, Caterpillar' and 'The Bird' link to the same theme. **PCM 56** is a diagram of an oak tree and its inhabitants for children to label using a word bank. **CD-ROM A**: *The Oak Tree* is a Talking Book. It includes three related activities and an opportunity for free writing.
Primary Framework objectives Foundation Stage Word recognition: Read some high frequency words; Hear and say sounds in words in the order in which they occur. Understanding and interpreting texts: Show an understanding of the elements of stories, such as main character, sequence of events, and openings, and how information can be found in non-fiction texts to answer questions about where, who, why and how. Listening and responding: Sustain attentive listening, responding to what they have heard by relevant comments, questions or actions. *Scottish 5–14 Strands:* Listening, Talking, Reading, Writing, Level A	for, we, like	breakfast, cake, yuk, chocolate, apple, yum, lunch	**PCM 57** provides further practice in reading key words introduced in the text, along with other common breakfast words. Encourage children to focus on the initial letters when matching words and pictures.

Book band	About the book	Text type	Curriculum links

Red B / Band 2B

My Exercise Diary

Alison Hawes and Steve Lumb

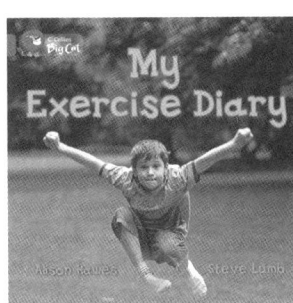

This non-fiction book recounts the different sporting activities enjoyed by a boy during one week. Photographs show the narrator having fun, engaged in different forms of exercise. Simple text reinforces the days of the week. A pictorial diary summary is included on pages 14 and 15.

A simple non-fiction recount

Early Learning Goals: Physical Development: Move with control and coordination; recognise the importance of keeping healthy; PSHE: Be confident to try new activities

Red B / Band 2B

Super Ben

Steve Smallman

This patterned picture story follows Ben on his trip to the park. The text describes the park visit, while the illustrations delve into Ben's imagination and reveal the adventures of "Super Ben". In Ben's imagination, Super Ben encounters a shark in the duck pond, a roundabout becomes a spaceship and puddles contain monsters! The labelled story map on pages 14 and 15 incorporates interest words from the text and some of Super Ben's encounters, encouraging children to follow Ben's adventures once more.

A patterned story with predictable structure

Early Learning Goals: Personal Social and Moral Development: Understand that there need to be codes of behaviour

Red B / Band 2B

What Are You Making?

Alison Hawes and Antony Elworthy

A non-fiction book about a group of children making a monster. Each stage of the monster-making process is shown – from the body and head, to the eyes, teeth and claws. Repetitive text asks what is being made, and then reveals the answer on the following page. The complete and labelled monster on page 14, and the separate labelled parts on page 15 remind children how the monster was put together.

A non-fiction recount

Early Learning Goals: Physical development: Handle materials safely and with increasing control. Creative Development: Explore colour, texture, shape, form and space in two and three dimensions; Use imagination in play; Express and communicate ideas, thoughts and feelings by designing and making

Learning objectives	High frequency words	Interest words	Related resources
Primary Framework objectives Foundation Stage Engaging with and responding to texts: Know that print carries meaning and, in English, is read from left to right and top to bottom. Word recognition: Read some high frequency words; Hear and say sounds in words in the order in which they occur; Read simple words by sounding out and blending the phonemes all through the word. Understanding and interpreting texts: Show an understanding of the elements of stories, such as main character, sequence of events, and openings, and how information can be found in non-fiction texts to answer questions about where, who, why and how. *Scottish 5–14 Strands:* Listening, Talking, Reading, Writing, Level A	on, I, went, had, to, the, all, we	exercise, Monday, Tuesday, Wednesday, skateboarding, Thursday, Friday, trampolining, Saturday, rollerblading, Sunday	**PCM 58** features a simple diary template for children to record their sporting activities on for one week, using words and/or pictures.
Primary Framework objectives Foundation Stage Word recognition/Word structure and spelling: Use phonic knowledge to write simple regular words and make phonetically plausible attempts at more complex words; Hear and say sounds in words in the order in which they occur. Understanding and interpreting texts: Retell narratives in the correct sequence, drawing on the language patterns of stories; Show an understanding of the elements of stories, such as main character, sequence of events, and openings, and how information can be found in non-fiction texts to answer question about where, who, why and how. *Scottish 5–14 Strands:* Listening, Talking, Reading, Writing, Level A	and, his, went, to, the, a, on, he, the, home, then, it, go, was, time, what, did, do	puddles, park, roundabout	**PCM 59**: Children fill in missing initial letters describing what Ben did in the park and draw their favourite Super Ben adventure.
Primary Framework objectives Foundation Stage Creating and shaping texts: Convey information and ideas in simple non-narrative forms Understanding and interpreting texts: Use syntax and context when reading for meaning; Make predictions from a brief look at covers, including blurb, title. Engaging with and responding to texts: Distinguish fiction and non-fiction texts and the different purposes for reading them. Word recognition: Recognition of high frequency words. Group discussion and interaction: Take turns to speak, listen to other's suggestions. *Scottish 5–14 Strands:* Listening, Talking, Reading, Writing, Level A	are, have, he, is, she, we, what, you	ping pong balls, rubbish bin, laundry basket, pen, funnel, shredded paper, feather boa, cardboard, crepe paper, egg carton, aluminium foil, feather dusters	**PCM 60**: Children draw their own monster and label it.

Collins Big Cat and the Scottish 5–14 Guidelines

Collins Big Cat's approach supports the early stages of children's reading development from P1–3. With its graded texts identified by colour, it introduces all the learning outcomes of Level A and B in a structured, well-organised way.

The fiction books provide a strong story line, supported by excellent illustrations. They contain familiar characters, settings and events to keep children interested and enthusiastic from the emergent readers to the more independent development readers in P3.

The non-fiction books are clear and accessible for young children. They contain superb photographs and illustrations supported by simple text and provide a development of all the necessary informational features required at this early stage.

The vocabulary is based on the most used common words and encourages use of phonics and rhyme.

It is a visual approach which promotes talking and listening and at the end of each book provides a visual recap to support writing from the early stages.

Guided reading practice supports the teaching approaches suggested in *Improving Reading at the Early Stages 5–14* (p13) where the teacher is encouraged to:

- *Listen to pupils talking about their experiences of reading*
- *Discuss stories, events and characters and relate these to pupils' own experiences*
- *Explain the context, where this is outside the pupil's experience*
- *Teach short phonic lessons e.g. emphasising initial letter sounds and recalling or comparing words with similar sounds in the text, looking at the endings of words and finding words which rhyme*
- *Revisit familiar/key words*
- *Introduce new reading vocabulary*
- *Ask pupils to read aloud to others in the group*

5–14 Strands	Lilac	Pink A	Pink B	Red A	Red B
Listening	Level A	Level A	Level A	Level A	Level A
For information instructions and directions	✓	✓	✓	✓	✓
In groups	✓	✓	✓	✓	✓
To respond to texts	✓	✓	✓	✓	✓
Awareness if genre	✓	✓	✓	✓	✓
Knowledge about language	✓	✓	✓	✓	✓
Talking	Level A	Level A	Level A	Level A	Level A
To convey information	✓	✓	✓	✓	✓
In groups	✓	✓	✓	✓	✓
About experiences feelings and opinions	✓	✓	✓	✓	✓
About texts	✓	✓	✓	✓	✓
Audience awareness	✓	l	✓	✓	✓
Knowledge about language	✓	✓	✓	✓	✓

Note: The writing activities for lilac, pink and red books should be led and modelled by the teacher.

- *Explain the meanings of words*
- *Discuss the effectiveness of the language used*
- *Explain some of the features of different types of text, for example of non-fiction or poetry*
- *Encourage pupils to talk about their favourite parts of stories or favourite characters*
- *Ask pupils to read back scribed stories or captions*
- *Use language games or story tapes*

The *Ideas for Guided Reading* at the back of each book clearly exemplify the learning opportunities and support the teacher in modelling good reading practice to their pupils. Children are often encouraged to work in pairs – to share ideas, pose questions, practise reading aloud with expression and intonation and develop a sense of character through role play. This approach is now recognised as a good learning strategy in an effective classroom.

The *Assessment and Support Guide* provides details on how to use the series and a title-by-title run through identifying learning objectives and links to the wider curriculum.

Collins Big Cat will greatly enhance and enrich any reading programme and build on the many language skills children require at this important stage of reading development. *Improving Reading at the Early Stages 5–14* states the importance of a challenging reading programme to stimulate pupils to extend their skills effectively during P3. There is no doubt that *Collins Big Cat* meets all of the necessary criteria.

"Where practice was best… pupils in P3 were beginning to:
- *Read more widely or at greater length, for example in reading short novels*
- *Read with increased fluency and expression*
- *Read to find evidence from a passage, to make simple inferences, to discuss the effectiveness of language and to identify main ideas*
- *Demonstrate their skills in understanding the language and structure of simple information passages such as descriptions, instructions and reports; and*
- *Discuss books and express their own responses in comments and book reviews."*
(Pg 4)

5–14 Strands	Lilac	Pink A	Pink B	Red A	Red B
Reading	Level A	Level A	Level A	Level A	Level A
For information	✓	✓	✓	✓	✓
For enjoyment	✓	✓	✓	✓	✓
To reflect on the writer's ideas and craft	✓	✓	✓	✓	✓
Awareness of genre	✓	✓	✓	✓	✓
Aloud		✓	✓	✓	✓
Knowledge about language	✓	✓	✓	✓	✓
Writing	Level A	Level A	Level A	Level A	Level A
Functional	✓	✓	✓	✓	✓
Personal		✓	✓	✓	✓
Imaginative	✓	✓	✓	✓	✓
Punctuation and structure					
Spelling				✓	✓
Handwriting and presentation				✓	✓
Knowledge about language	✓	✓	✓	✓	✓

Note: The writing activities for lilac, pink and red books should be led and modelled by the teacher.

Put the pictures in the right order to tell the story.

Cat and Dog
Learning objective: Track the book in the right order

© HarperCollins*Publishers* 2005. This page may be photocopied for use in the classroom.

Name _____

Put the pictures in the right order to tell the story.

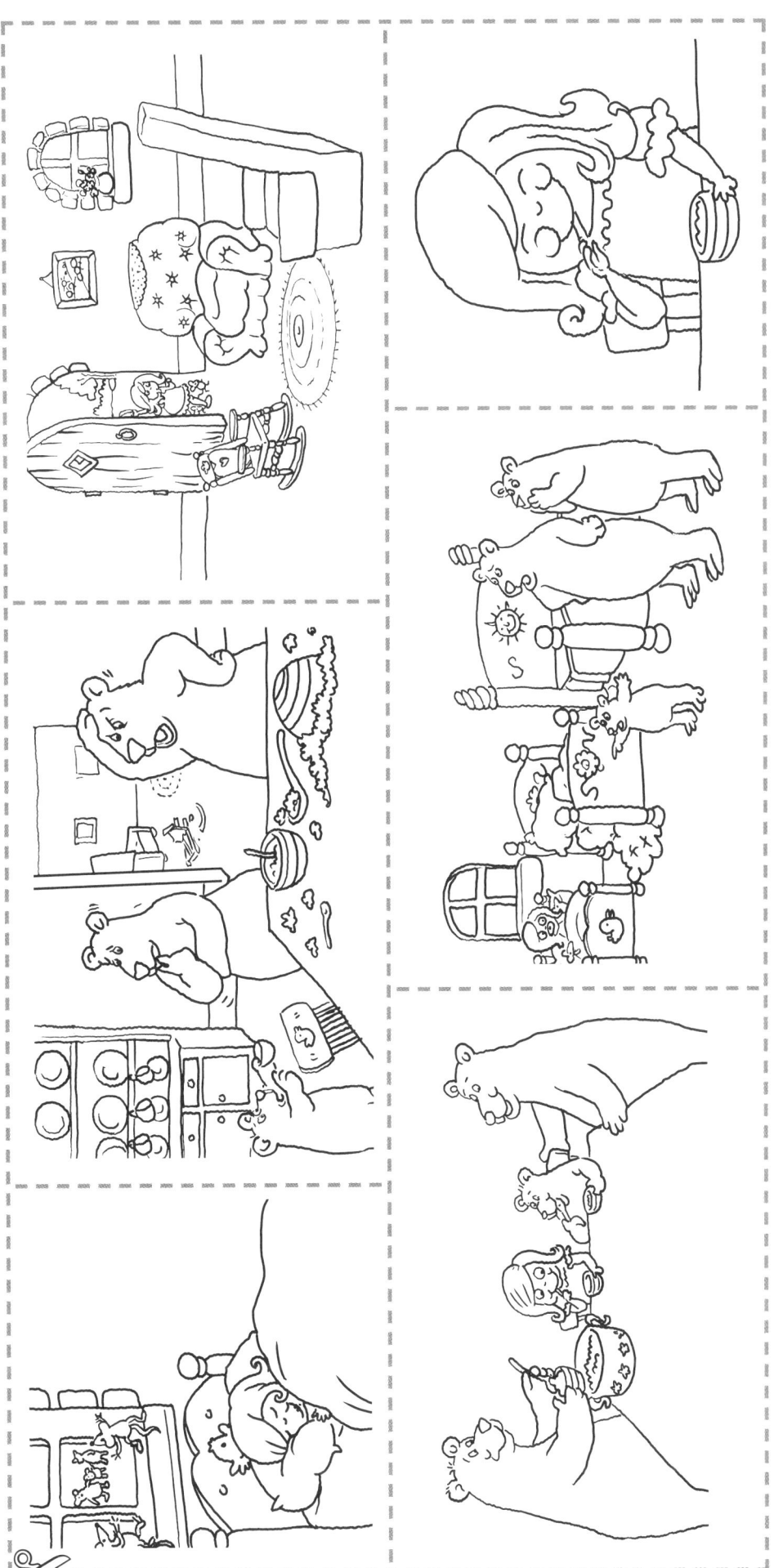

Goldilocks and the Three Bears

Learning objective: Track the text in the right order.

Name _____

Draw how the monkeys get the fruit.

| 1 | 2 | 3 |

Get the Fruit!

Learning objective: showing awareness of story structure

Name _____

Granny is late again.

Draw and write where she is going.

Oh dear me, I'm late for _____!

Oh dear me, I'm late for _____!

Oh Dear Me, I'm Late for Tea!

Learning objective: Using knowledge of familiar texts to re-enact or re-tell to others.

© HarperCollins*Publishers* 2005. This page may be photocopied for use in the classroom.

71

Name _____

Cut out the pictures.

Put them in the right order.

My Party

Learning objective: Sequencing events

Name _____

 Collins *Big Cat*

Draw stripes on each picture.

A zebra with stripes.

A snake with stripes.

A car with stripes.

A jumper with stripes.

Draw something else with stripes.

A _____ with stripes.

Stripes

Learning objective: Use knowledge of text to identify theme

© HarperCollins*Publishers* 2005. This page may be photocopied for use in the classroom.

Name _____

Collins Big Cat

Match the animals to their babies.

kangaroo

cygnet

chimpanzee

cat

alligator

young chimp

joey

swan

kitten

baby alligator

Carry Me
Learning objective: Identifying key themes and main points of text

Name _____

Finish the story.

1

2

3

4

Look Out, Butterfly!

Learning objective: Use knowledge of text to re-tell narrative

Name _____

Collins
Big Cat

Cut out the pictures.
Put them in the right order to tell the story.

The Big Turnip

Learning objective: retelling stories, ordering events using story language

Name _____

Design a scarecrow.

What will you use? Tick the boxes.

 football ☐

 balloon ☐

 straw hat ☐

 bamboo canes ☐

 paints ☐

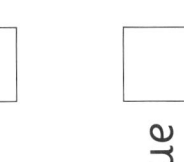 gloves ☐

 string ☐

 flowerpot ☐

 glue ☐

 shirt ☐

Draw a picture of your scarecrow.

How to Make a Scarecrow

Learning objective: using a non-fiction text to plan a design

© HarperCollins*Publishers* 2006.

This page may be photocopied for use in the classroom.

Name _____

Put the pictures in the right order to tell the story.

Stop That Robot

Learning objective: Track the book in the right order.

Name _____

Match the people to their jobs.

What am I?

Learning objective: How information in non-fiction texts can answer questions about who, why and how.

Name _____

Collins
Big Cat

Fill in the lines to tell the story.

| grass | tent | bath | mud | sandpit | leaves |

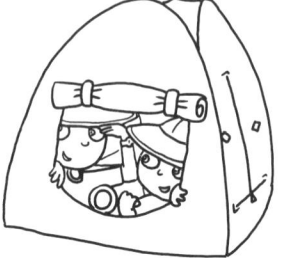

In the _____.

In the _____.

In the _____.

In the _____.

In the _____.

In the _____.

In the Garden
Learning objective: Understanding story structure; using picture cues

Name _____

PCM
14

Finish the story.

| pond | car | mud | garden | park |

In the _____.

In the _____.

In the _____.

In the _____.

In the _____.

The Very Wet Dog

Learning objective: Retelling story; using picture cues

Name _____

Join the dinosaurs to the instruments they play.

drum

guitar

piano

trumpet

flute

Dinosaur Rock
Learning objective: Using cues to read words

Name _____

Label the pictures.

| the rug | the drinks | the basket | the wasps |
| the cakes | the sandwiches |

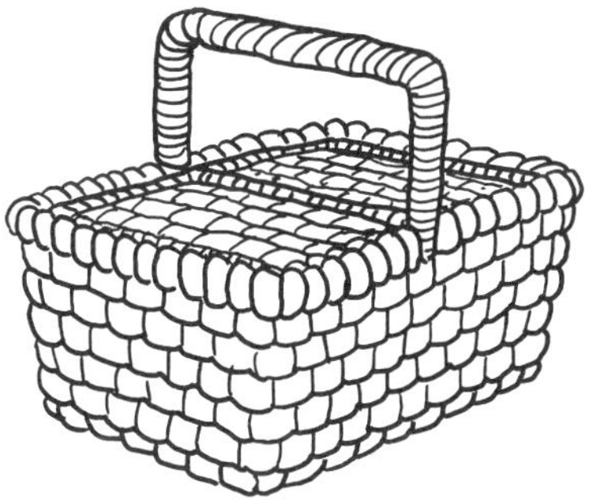

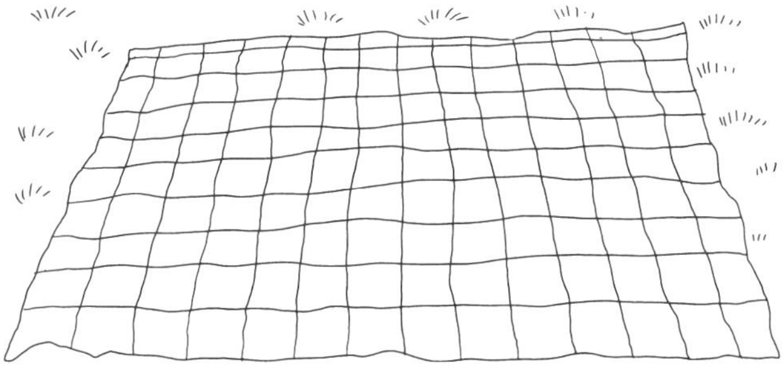

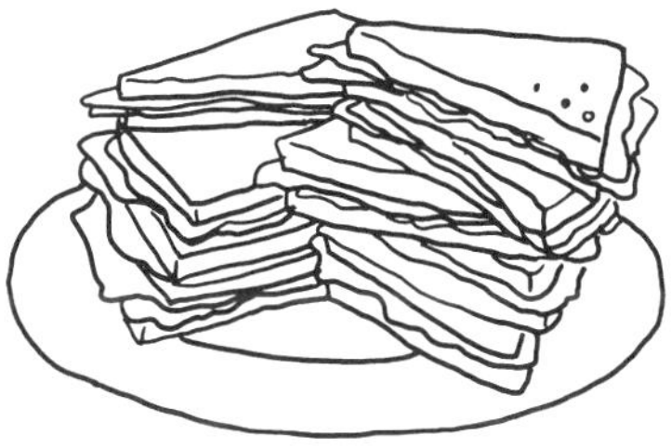

Name _____

Fill in the missing letters.

c	w	b	sn	l	sp

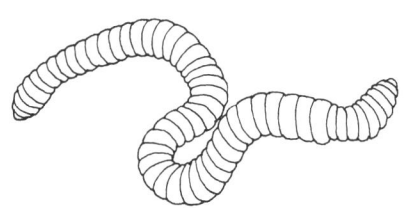

A _orm.

A _aterpillar.

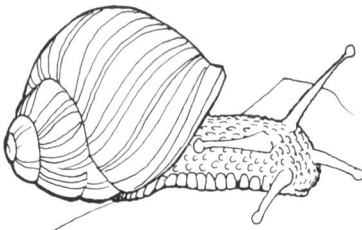

A ___ail.

A _utterfly.

A _adybird.

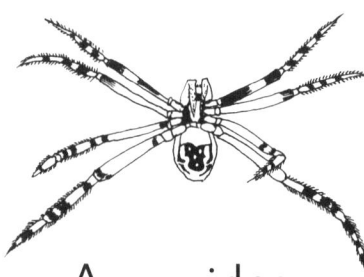

A ___ider.

Draw your favourite minibeast.

_____

Minibeasts
Learning objective: Using a variety of cues

Name _____

Read the labels and colour the cars.

yellow

green

black

blue

red

white

I like the _____ car best.

Name _____

Write **pushing** or **pulling** in each space.

I am _____.

I am _____.

I am _____.

I am _____.

Pushing and Pulling
Learning objective: Using picture cues

Name _____

Finish the poster labels.

My Skateboard

Name _____

Where are the guinea pigs?

Write the missing words and tell the story.

car   cage   garden   park

In the _____.

In the _____.

In the _____.

In the _____.

The Guinea Pigs

Learning objective: recounting main points of the story

Name _____

Look for shapes in the picture.

Join each word to a matching shape.

circle

triangle

star

square

rectangle

hexagon

Shapes

Learning objective: reading shape words on sight

Name _____

Read the words and label the pictures.

| mouse rabbits cats dogs elephants fish |

One _____   Two _____

Three _____   Four _____

Five _____   Six _____

In the Boat
Learning objective: Extend vocabulary through meaning and sounds of new words.
© HarperCollins*Publishers* 2007. This page may be photocopied for use in the classroom.

Name _____

How many animals are there in each picture?

Match the number to the picture.

1 one

2 two

3 three

4 four

5 five

6 six

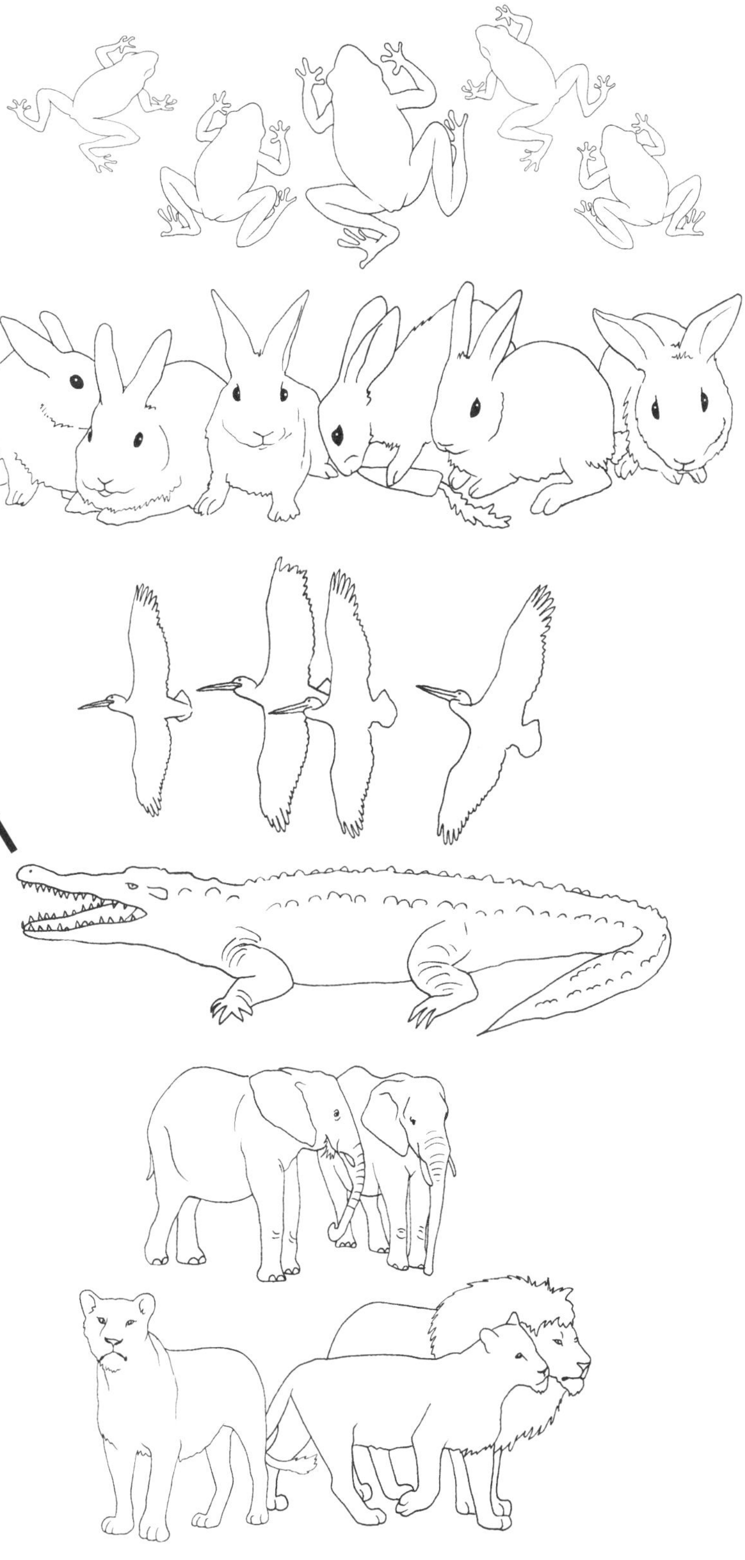

How Many Animals?

Learning objective: How information in non-fiction texts can answer questions about who, why and how.

Name _____

Collins
Big Cat

Who is on the see-saw with Hippo? Draw each one.

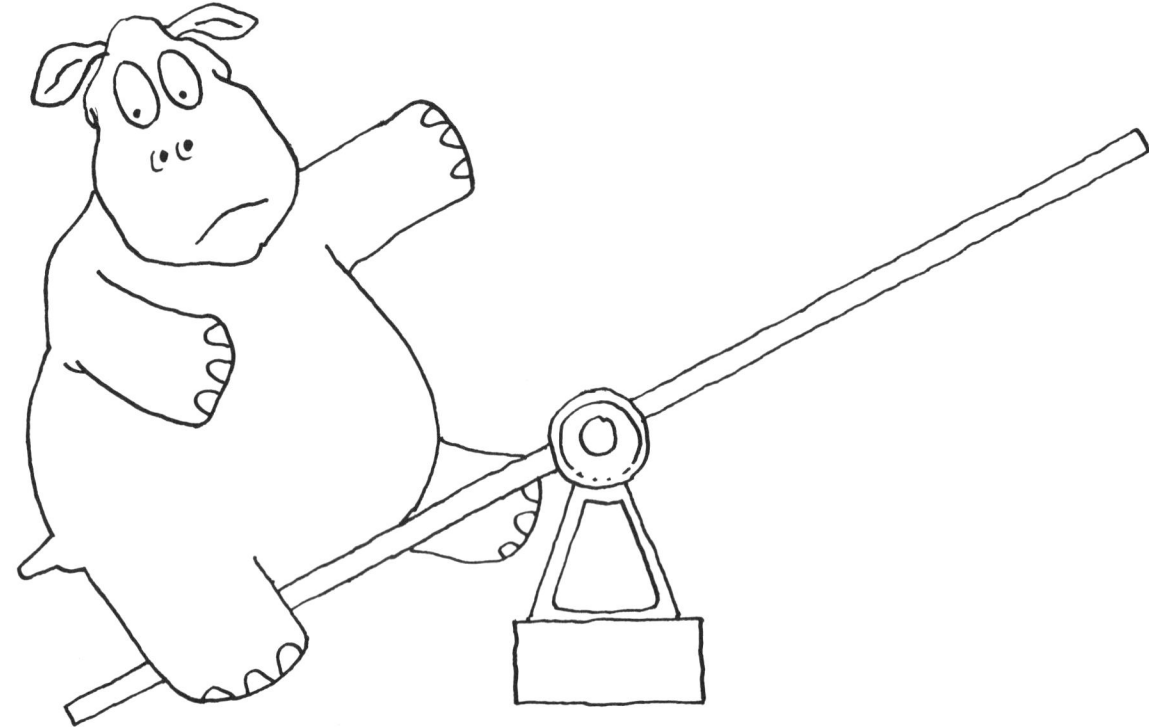

_____ is lighter than Hippo.

_____ is heavier than Hippo.

The See-saw
Learning objective: Awareness of story structure: action and reaction

Name _____

In the bath

Use these words to label the picture.

| flippers | shark | boat | goggles | armbands |

The Big Splash
Learning objective: Using labels

© HarperCollins*Publishers* 2005.
This page may be photocopied for use in the classroom.

Name _____

Write labels for the robot.

head	foot	hand	arm	leg	body

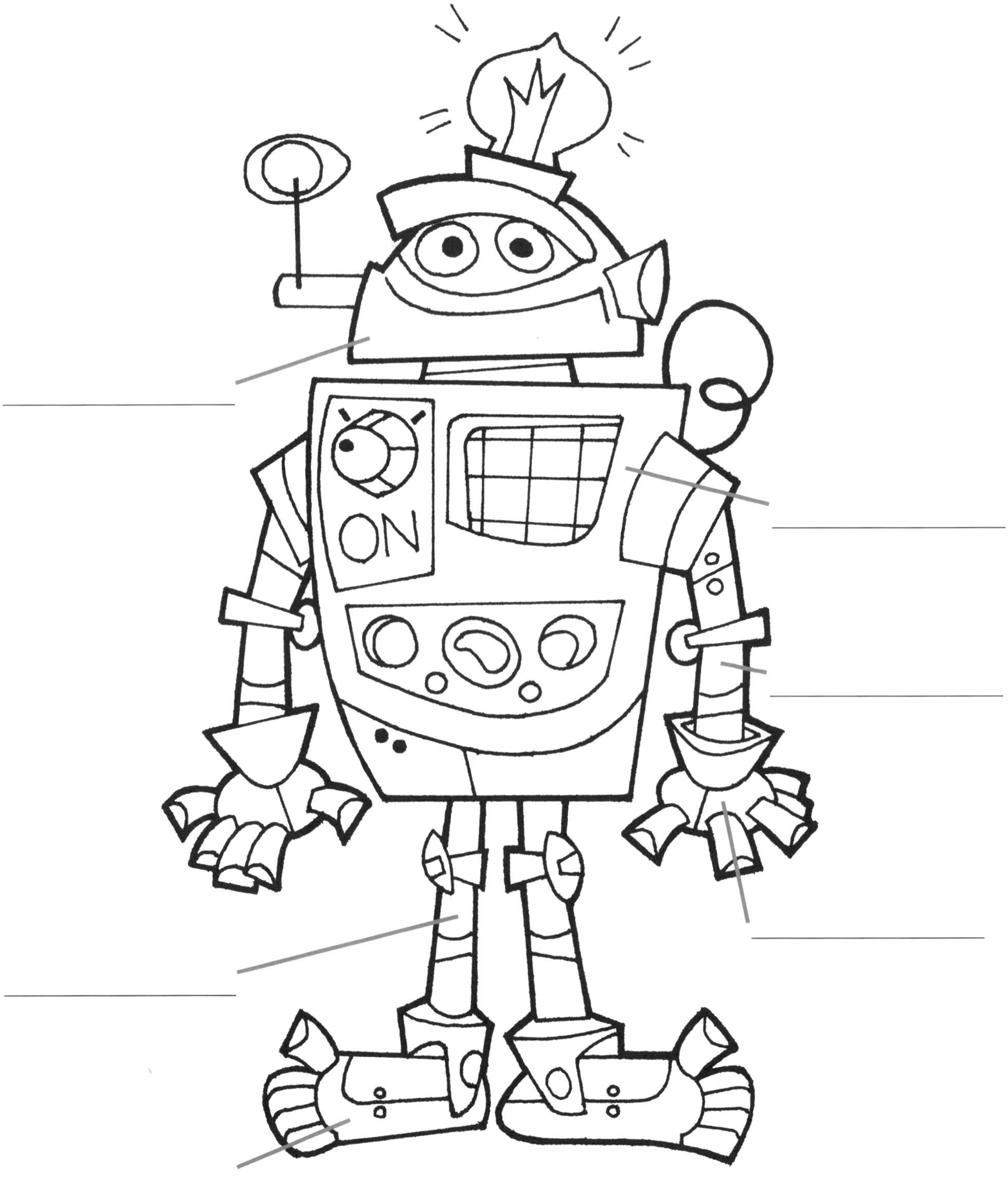

The Robot

Learning objective: Using labels

Name _____

Fill in the missing letters.

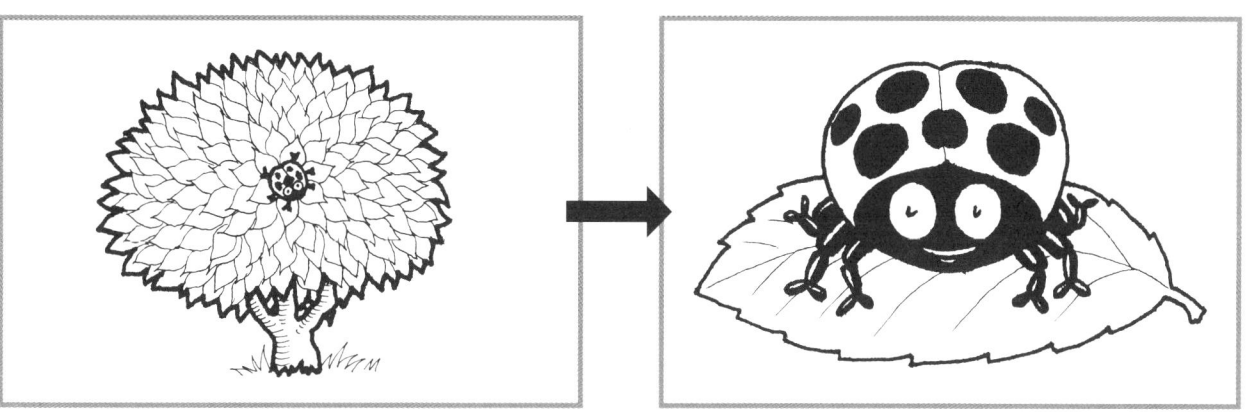

Ladybird is on the __ __ee.

Ladybird is on the __eaf.

Ladybird is on the __ond.

Finish the drawing.

Ladybird is on the __ __ower.

Ladybird is home at last.

Fly Away Home

Learning objective: Identifying initial sounds and phonemes

Name _____

What did you find in the pond?

Fill in the names and numbers.

How does it look?	What is it called?	How many did you see?
	dragonfly	
	pond-skater	

The Pond

Learning objective: Observe and record features of the natural world

© HarperCollins*Publishers* 2005. This page may be photocopied for use in the classroom.

Name _____

Write labels for the wheels.

| slow | fat | big | small | fast | thin |

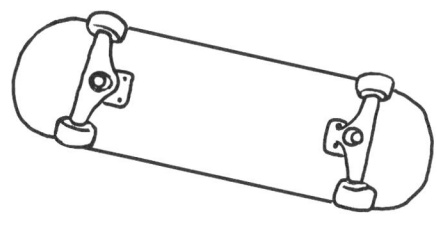

Wheels
Learning objective: Using labels

Name _____

Make a poster. Draw your favourite performer.

COME TO THE Circus

Date: _____
Time: _____
Place: _____

with: _____

Come to the Circus

Learning objective: Understand features of an event

Name _____

Draw lines to join the labels to the wild cat.

fur

tail

legs

ears

eyes

teeth

Cats
Learning objective: Using labels

© HarperCollins*Publishers* 2005.
This page may be photocopied for use in the classroom.

Name _____

Collins
Big Cat

Read the labels and colour the paint pots.

Red

Blue

Orange

Yellow

Green

Brown

What colour are the bears making? Tick the box.

green ☐   purple ☐   orange ☐

green ☐   purple ☐   orange ☐

Colour Bears
Learning objective: reading colour words on sight

© HarperCollins*Publishers* 2006. This page may be photocopied for use in the classroom.

Name _____

Find out which fruit is the most popular.

Tick the fruits you like. Then ask your friends which fruits they like. Fill in the chart.

	Me	_____	_____	_____
apples				
bananas				
grapes				
oranges				
melons				
strawberries				

We Like Fruit
Learning objective: recognising printed words; interacting with others

Name _____

Label the shapes on the monster.

| spots   stripes   squares   zigzags   triangles |

[Five labelling boxes connected to the monster illustration]

Monster Mess
Learning objective: Writing labels.

© HarperCollins*Publishers* 2007. This page may be photocopied for use in the classroom.

Name _____

Fill in the missing letters.

I'm __unning fast.

I'm __kating across.

I'm __reeping slowly.

I'm __umping up.

I'm __anging on.

I'm __wimming along.

What is your favourite activity?

My favourite activity is _____.

I Can Do It!
Learning objective: Identify initial sounds

Name _____

Finish the story by drawing and writing.

Bill went over a river.

The bear fell in the river.

He went up a hill.

The bear _____.

He went into a wood.

The bear _____.

He went to the bin.

The bear _____.

A Day Out

Learning objective: Recounting main points of the story

Name _____

Put the pictures in the right order to follow Tec's trail.

the dog

the cat

the hamster

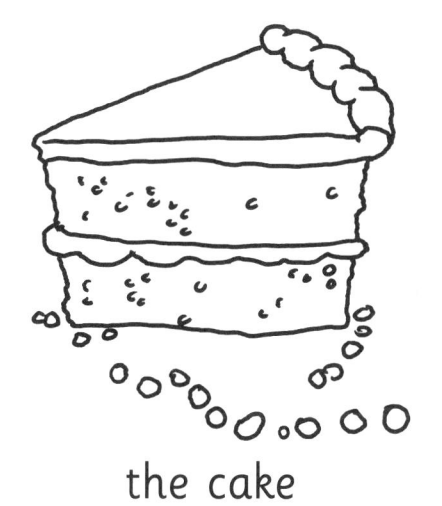

the cake

the fish

Name _____

Tec and the Hole

Design a new cover.

C Collins
Big Cat

Tec and the
Hole

C Collins
Big Cat

Tec and the
Hole

Tony Mitton
Martin Chatterton

Draw and write what the children saw.

1	2

seagulls   ice-cream van

3	4

_____   sand

5	6

sea   _____

Name _____

Shapes

Draw and label objects that match these shapes.

rectangle	ruler
circle	
star	
oval	
spiral	

Shapes on the Seashore
Learning objective: Collecting words related to shape

Name _____

Draw pictures and write labels to show what's inside.

What's inside this shed?

What's inside this fridge?

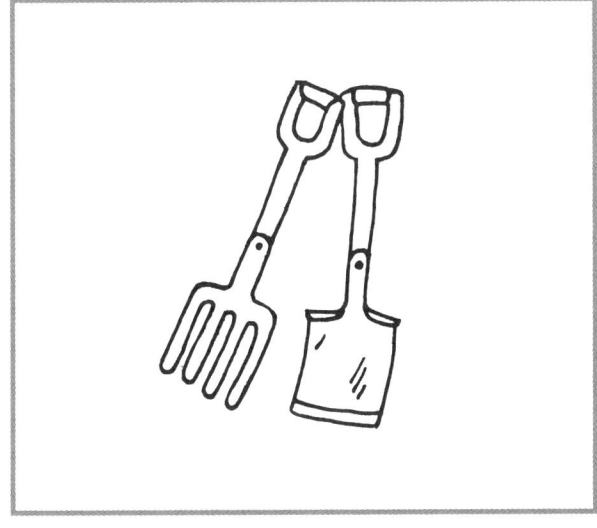

garden tools

_____

What's inside this washing machine?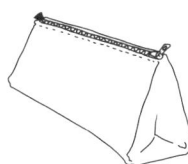

What's inside this pencil case?

_____   _____

Name _____

Fill in the letters.

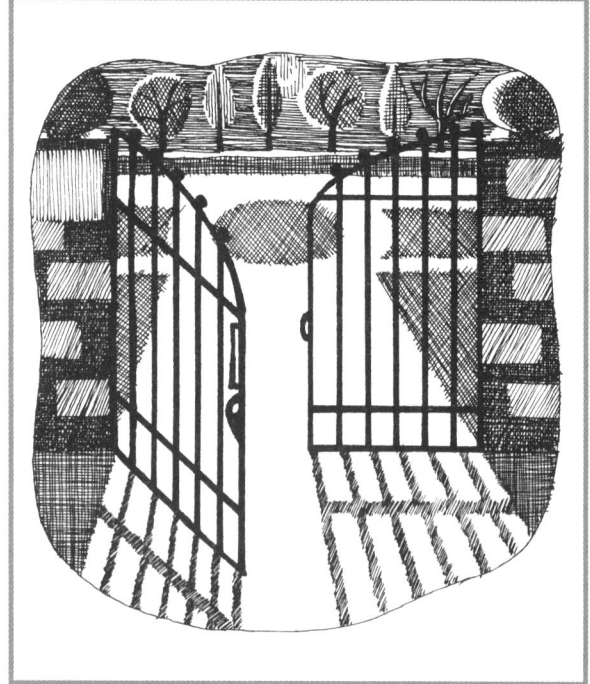

It is dark in the __ark.

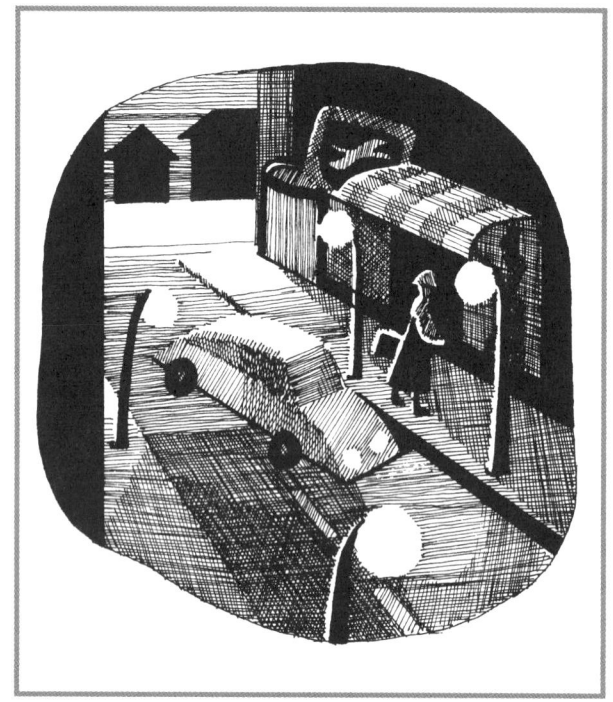

It is dark in the __treet.

It is dark in the __ood.

Draw your own picture.

It is dark in the _____.

In the Dark
Learning objective: Initial sounds

Name _____

Complete the sentences.

The red balloon goes up, up and away.

It goes over the _____

It goes over the _____

It goes over the _____

Up, Up and Away
Learning objective: Recounting events in order

Name _____

Collins
Big Cat

Where is Cat?

Read the questions. Write yes or no in each space.

Is Cat on the table?

_____

Is Cat behind the chair?

_____

Is Cat under the bed?

_____

Is Cat in the sink?

_____

Cat and Dog Play Hide and Seek
Learning objective: reading, checking for sense and responding

What things did the children see on the bike ride?

Draw them on the map.

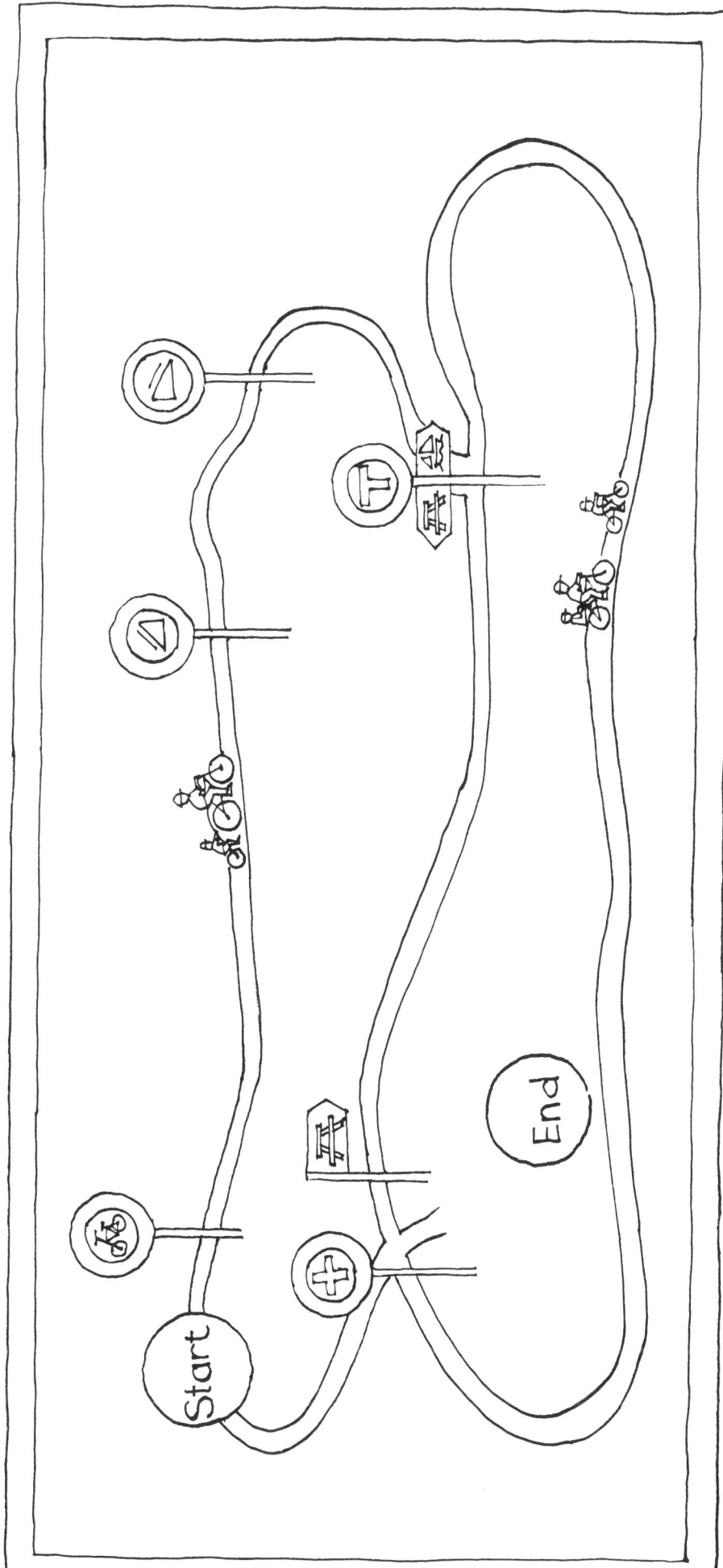

My Bike Ride

Learning objective: using knowledge of a text to present information on a map

Name _____

Which parts of the body would you use?

Match the picture to the <u>underlined</u> word.

Have you ever <u>seen</u> me?

Have you ever <u>heard</u> me?

Have you ever <u>smelt</u> me?

Have you ever <u>touched</u> me?

Have you ever <u>tasted</u> me?

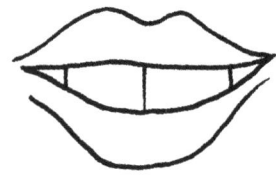

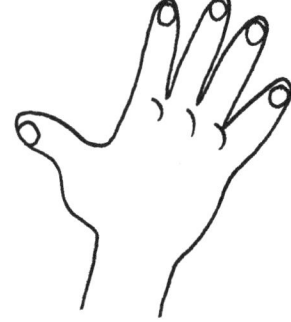

Have You Ever?

Learning objective: Use language to imagine and recreate roles and experiences.

Collins
Big Cat

PCM
48

Draw or write what the weather was like on each day.

Sunday	Monday
sunny	_____

Tuesday	Wednesday
rainy	_____

Thursday	Friday and Saturday
_____	snowy

What day is it today?

Today is _____.

What is the weather like today?

The weather is _____.

Weather Report
Learning objective: Use language to recreate experiences. Combine words with images.

Name _____

Cut out the labels.

Paste them in the right boxes.

the ship

the cave

✂ the beach ┆ the river ┆ the trees ┆ the hill

Pirates

Learning objective: Using reading cues to place labels

© HarperCollins*Publishers* 2005. This page may be photocopied for use in the classroom.

Name _____

Collins
Big Cat

Finish the story.

Mole said,

"Hello, Bee. Did you see the wind?"

Bee said, "_____."

Mole said,

"Hello, Mouse. Did you see the wind?"

_____ said, "_____."

Mole said,

"Hello, Deer. Did you see the _____?"

_____ said, "_____."

Where is the Wind?
Learning objective: Checking written text makes sense

Name _____

Write and draw what you will do on each day.

Monday	Tuesday	Wednesday	Thursday

Friday	Saturday	Sunday	

Woody's Week

Learning objective: Organising and sequencing events by day of the week.

Name _____

Collins
Big Cat

Litter survey

Investigate litter in your school playground.

What did you find?	How many did you find?
crisp packet	
drink carton	
sweet wrapper	
_____	
_____	

I found _____ pieces of litter altogether.

Name _____

Sort it!

Draw arrows to show where
the things should go.

Cardboard

Glass

Leaves

Paper

Wood

At the Dump

Learning objective: Show knowledge and understanding of the text.

Name _____

Collins
Big Cat

Draw and write what you like to eat.

Breakfast

_____

_____

Lunch

_____

_____

Dinner

_____

_____

Name _____

Draw lines to show where you would go to buy things.

| eggs |

| trainers |

| grapes |

| bread |

| book |

| comic |

| drink |

Let's Go Shopping
Learning objective: Understanding features of the place you live in

Name _____

Use the words in the box to write labels for the animals in the oak tree.

bat	fox	ant	rabbit	wasp	mole

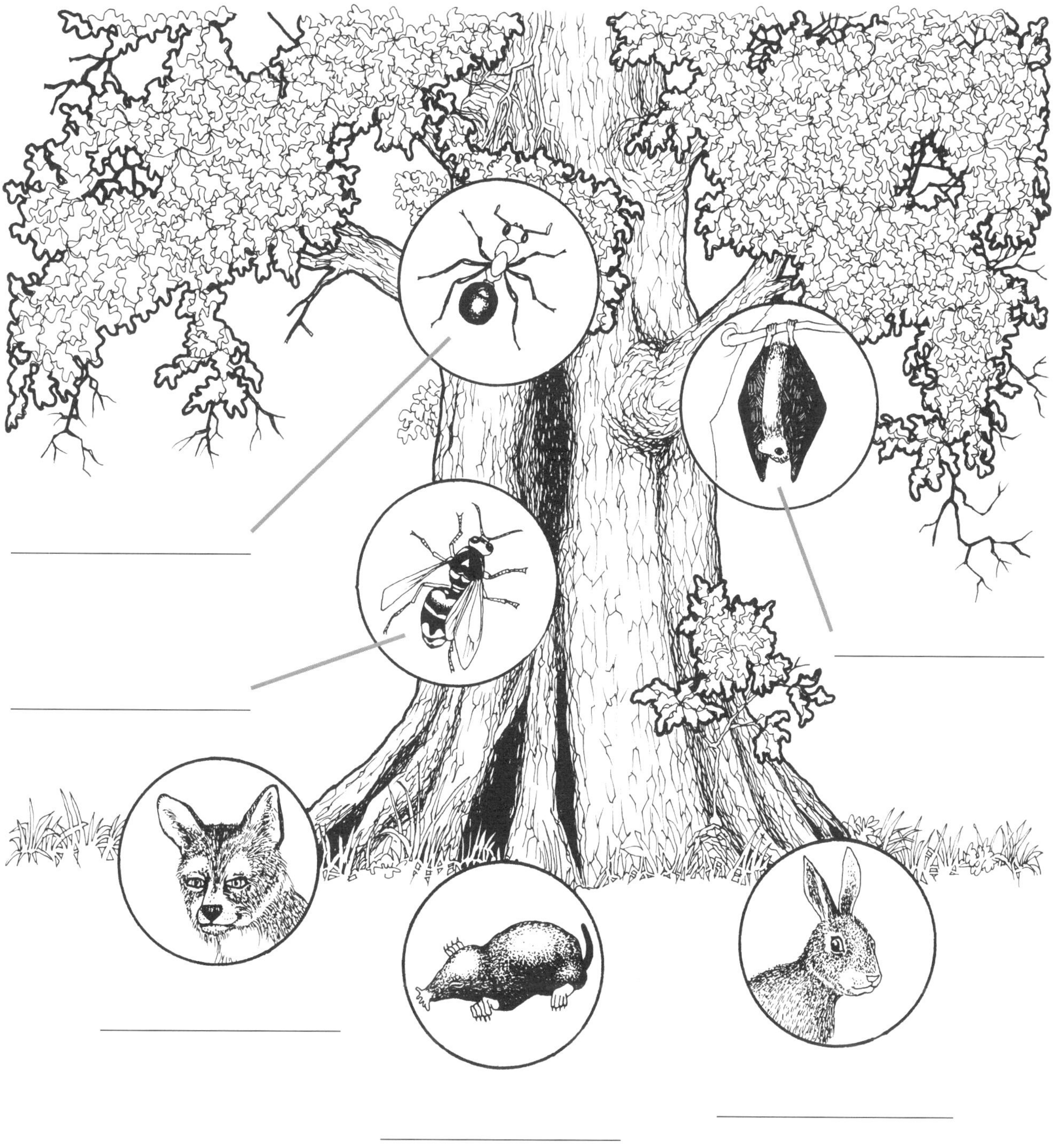

_____

_____

_____

_____

_____

The Oak Tree

Learning objective: Using labels

123

Name _____

What's for breakfast?

Join each picture to the correct word.

apple

egg

toast

yogurt

cake

chocolate

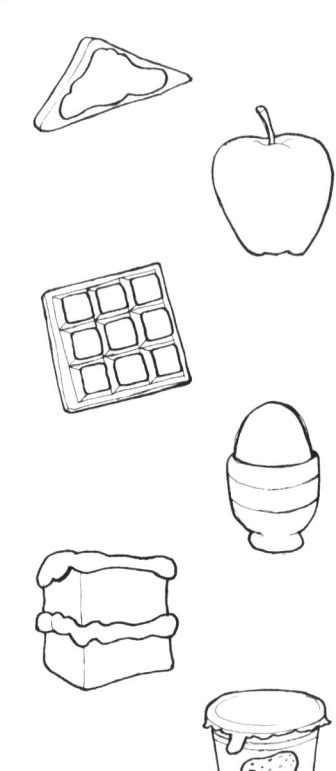

What did you eat for breakfast today?

_____

_____

_____

What's for Breakfast?

Learning objective: reading familiar words independently

© HarperCollins*Publishers* 2006. This page may be photocopied for use in the classroom.

Name _____

Keep an exercise diary.
Draw or write what you
do each day.

Monday

Tuesday

Wednesday

Thursday

Friday

Saturday

Sunday

My Exercise Diary

Learning objective: reading high frequency words; recording information in a chart

Name _____

Fill in the missing letters.

Ben went to the __ark.

Ben fed the __ucks.

Ben played on the __oundabout.

Ben __ __lashed in the puddles.

Draw your favourite Super Ben adventure.

Super Ben
Learning objective: Identify initial sounds

Name _____

Draw your own monster.

Label it with these words:

| head | body | eyes | teeth | claws |

What Are You Making?

Learning objective: Convey information and ideas in simple non-narrative forms.

127

© HarperCollins*Publishers* 2007. This page may be photocopied for use in the classroom.

Collins Big Cat and guided reading

What is guided reading?

A guided reading lesson usually takes place with a teacher and a small group of children at roughly the same attainment level. It is a vital part of the teaching of reading, being the step between shared reading with explicit reading instruction and independent reading.

The lesson revolves around one book, with each child in the group having their own copy. After a book introduction by the teacher the children are expected to read independently. The expectation is that the children will *apply* their knowledge and experience of texts and reading strategies gained in the shared reading sessions.

Selecting the right book for the group's reading level and interest level is vital. In the context of guided reading, the children should be able to read about 90% of the text easily. The remaining 10% of the book presents a challenge to the children and offers a focused teaching and learning opportunity which forms the basis of the guided reading lesson. The book can also reflect the childrens' learning needs assessed prior to choosing the book. In this way the children read comfortably with comprehension, while

developing specific reading strategies. *Collins Big Cat* supports selection of the correct book by banding each book to show the reading level it requires.

A guided reading session generally comprises four parts:

1. **Getting started**: The *introduction to the new book*, led by the teacher, which paves the way for the children's independent reading of the book.

2. **Reading and responding**: The *independent reading of the book* by each child, monitored by the teacher who prompts the children to problem solve challenges within the book.

3. **Returning to the text**: A *re-reading of the book*, led by the teacher, prompting discussion of the group's response and a re-cap of specific learning objectives.

4. **Checking and moving on**: A *follow-up activity* that consolidates the learning objectives of the guided reading session. It can be a group activity or an activity to do in pairs or individually.

Of course, every book is different, but here are some guidelines to approaching a guided reading session. These guidelines have been adopted by

Collins Big Cat, and every title has a suggested guided reading plan at the back (*Ideas for guided reading*).

1. Getting started

The book introduction is a key part of the guided reading session. It works best if you know the book reasonably well, and are aware where challenges may arise, as well as the learning objectives to focus on.

You may choose to introduce concepts in the book by looking at a prop or very short activity together with the group. For example, show the children classroom instruments as an introduction to *Dinosaur Rock* (Pink A/Band 1A). This prompts the children to think about instruments and performing, and so supports their understanding of the story.

Read the title aloud and discuss it with the group. The title and cover gives lots of information about what the book might be about and develops the children's skills of prediction and activates their prior knowledge of the context/content thus enhancing comprehension. The purpose of this part is to familiarise the children with the text and its structure thus reducing uncertainty.

Walk the children through the book, page by page, talking about the events in your own words. Encourage the children to look at the pictures and 'read' the story through the illustrations. As you talk about the events in the book, use the style and language of the book – this helps to prepare the children, familiarising them with the book before they read it independently. You could introduce tricky words and specialist or interest vocabulary, perhaps with word cards, pointing out where they occur in the text.

2. Reading and responding

Returning to the beginning of the book, this time the children read the story by themselves while you observe and monitor them. One or two key questions can be posed for the children to find out as they read. Tell them what you are expecting them to do and what you expect to see. The children read quietly, at their own pace. During the children's independent reading, intervene when appropriate to prompt/teach reading skills explicitly. For example, you might ask children about the strategies they are using, or prompt children to use strategies to problem-solve any challenges they encounter. Encourage children to solve challenges for themselves without you giving the answer. You could prompt them to use reading strategies they have learned from the shared reading sessions, and praise reading strategies when they are used.

3. Returning to the book

When the children have finished reading independently, talk about the book together. Use opportunities to consolidate learning objectives, follow up discussion about the story or characters and to recap on events, checking children's overall comprehension of plot and sequence, for example by asking them to retell events in their own words or hot-seating as a character. Return to the questions posed and to specific parts of the text to check comprehension.

4. Checking and moving on

At the end of the guided reading session, the main focus should be on reinforcing the main learning objectives. It is also an opportunity to meaningfully link the guided reading session to work done in the rest of the class. The conclusion of the guided session could set children an activity that both draws on the work done in the session and links to the work in the wider classroom. The activity can be done as a group activity, in pairs or independently, and may link naturally to other areas of the curriculum – for example, Music, Art or Science. *Ideas for guided reading* at the back of every *Collins Big Cat* book provide a range of ideas for follow-up activities. This Assessment and Support Guide also provides photocopy masters for further activities (see pp68–127).

Collins Big Cat book bands and progression

The key to successful guided reading sessions is skilful selection of the appropriate text for a particular child or group of children. Each book should provide neither too little nor too much challenge for the reader.

The goal of guided reading is for children to read accurately, with enjoyment, putting into practice appropriate reading strategies while thinking about the meaning of the book. Within the context of guided reading, if the book presents too much of a challenge (e.g. where the child makes more than one error in every ten words) then the child's reading may lose fluency, phrasing and motivation. If the book presents too little challenge then the child is not reading at an appropriate level for making progress.

Collins Big Cat supports teachers by grading each book clearly. *Collins Big Cat* books are graded into 20 bands of progressive difficulty, from the simplest wordless books at Lilac/0 level to books for fluent readers at Diamond/20.* These bands are similar to the level by level rationale of *Book Bands for Guided Reading* (Bickler, Baker and Hobsbaum, UK Reading Recovery National Network). *Collins Big Cat* banding helps the teacher to match suitable reading books to a child's reading ability level, invaluable in planning guided reading sessions. There is a bookbanding summary from Lilac/0 to Lime/11 on the inside back cover of this guide.

Managing progression in guided reading

Guided reading works most effectively when the children in a group are working at a similar level on an appropriate book which offers the right

Collins Big Cat book bands at Upper Foundation/Scottish P1 stage

Working towards National Curriculum Level 1

Scottish 5–14 Guidelines Level A (reading, talking, writing, listening)

Book band	Learning opportunities	Text features	Approximate word count
Lilac Band 0	Locate title and open front cover Relates narrative to own experience Retells narrative using own words	Wordless book Illustration provides full support for telling story / narrative	0
Pink A Band 1A	Locate title, open front cover and turn pages Understand we read left-right Matches spoken to printed word (one-to-one matching) Locate familiar words to help check reading Predict storyline and some vocabulary	Language follows children's speech patterns Repetitive sentence structure includes high frequency words Illustration provides full, direct support for text Further illustration provides support for speaking and listening 2-4 words per page	14-20
Pink B Band 1B	As Pink A but offering slightly more challenge	4-6 words per page	20-30
Red A Band 2A	Consolidate one-to-one matching Use known words to check reading Read with phrasing while keeping track of text Repeat text to check or change own reading Predict from meaning, syntax and print to solve new words	Sentences short with children's language patterns Repetitive phrase and sentence structures Highly predictable text, simple story development Illustration provides full, direct support for text Further illustration provides support for speaking and listening	30-40
Red B Band 2B	As Red A but offering slightly more challenge	As Red A but offering slightly more challenge May be more than one line per page	40-60

Collins Big Cat books at Sapphire/19 and Diamond/20 coming soon – see www.collinsbigcat.com for more details.

amount of challenge. Careful assessment enables the teacher to put the children into ability groups and to identify the appropriate level of *Collins Big Cat* for each group.

Children enter school with varying levels of reading ability and experience of reading. Some children come into class already reading. Others will be working towards being able to do this by the end of the summer term.

An effective way of assessing which band is appropriate for a child is by filling in a **Reading Skills sheet** (see pp138 to 140) as the child reads a book at a level which you consider most suits their reading experience. These sheets outline the reading skills a child should be able to demonstrate at each book band. High scores in most of these categories suggest the child be placed at a higher band, average or low scores that the child should continue in this band or even move to an easier band.

Checking progression

Children make progress at different rates and often in spurts. Useful indicators of how suited children are to a reading level are:

- fluency in reading
- comprehension of the book they are reading
- number of miscues when reading unfamiliar words.

A child's progress in these skills can be checked in the **Reading Skills sheets** (see pp138 to 140) at regular intervals. These sheets provide a basis for you to observe and assess which skills the child has mastered and which still need to be developed or consolidated, and decide whether the child should move bands. They also give you the opportunity to identify and intervene where a particular weakness is holding back a child's progress.

It is a good idea to periodically re-check each child's reading skills using these or your own school's sheets every six weeks or so, and re-group

or re-band children if necessary. A child who reads fluently and with comprehension at their current level, making few if any miscues, might be moved up a level. A child who is struggling with the book and losing the sense of what they read might be moved down a level.

Additionally, if you are keeping continuous assessment records during each guided reading session, (e.g. by using the **Ongoing Records** provided on pp135–137) this can also be used to check the child's reading level and appropriate band.

Collins Big Cat bands

Collins Big Cat Lilac/0 is ideal for those children who are beginning to find out about reading but are not ready to read books with words. These wordless books can be used for demonstrating book handling skills, providing rich language experiences, and developing visual literacy. They support learning about story sequencing and prediction skills, and provide a stimulus for discussing story structures and drawing on the child's prior knowledge and experience.

From *Collins Big Cat* Pink/1 onwards, the books support the teaching of one to one correspondence between spoken and written words. Pink A books have two to three words per spread, with highly patterned text and a good picture cue for support. The books become progressively more complex, with short sentences on most pages by Red B. Again the books provide opportunities for rich language experiences and developing visual literacy through the illustrations, which extend the story and are an essential part of the text. They support learning about story sequencing and prediction skills, and provide a stimulus for discussing book structures and features of fiction and non-fiction, and for drawing on the child's prior knowledge and experience.

Ideas for assessment

The key to good assessment is to identify each child's strengths and weaknesses followed by immediate intervention and/or further teaching. The photocopiable assessment and planning sheets provided in the *Collins Big Cat Assessment and Support Guide* are designed to help with this.

What is reading assessment?

Assessment of a child's reading begins with observations of their response to books, their knowledge of phonics and punctuation and their enthusiasm and interest in reading. Nursery assessment records may clarify for Reception/P1 teachers whether or not a child is ready to work in a guided reading group. For example, can the child open a book without tearing it, understand that pictures tell a story, and concentrate for periods of about fifteen minutes?

Preparing for the reading session

Before working with a book in a guided reading session, it is important to identify which learning opportunities are offered by it, and what you will be looking for in children's reading and response to the book. *Collins Big Cat* books have learning objectives and ideas for guided reading provided at the back of every book in the *Ideas for guided reading* section. When using the books with a guided reading group, you can refer to this to help you assess, for example, children's use of phonic and picture clues, and their understanding of the author's meaning.

During the reading session

Although assessment should be continuous, only significant strengths and weaknesses need to be noted for each child, related to what is being taught. Many weaknesses can be corrected immediately by good intervention from teachers. For example, open questions and involving dialogue help children to think about their learning and their next steps for improvement. Remember that most small children need time to respond to open questions beginning *What if… ? How would you… ? Why do you think…?* When necessary, reassure them by saying *Think about it: I'll come back to you in a moment.*

After the reading session

Used systematically and analytically, *Collins Big Cat* assessment stimulates reading progress by focusing planning on the significant weaknesses of individual children and/or groups. Identified weaknesses can be rectified **between** guided reading sessions by one-to-one intervention from teachers, teaching assistants, or by homework and parental help. Intervention is essential to the assessment process. It increases children's reading confidence, and accelerates learning in the time available for guided reading.

Remember that children may progress at different rates. Continuous assessment helps you to identify when attainment groups need to be re-formed, as will happen from time to time. For example, where some children in a starter reading group can recognise their own names and familiar words, others may need continuing picture book experiences.

Progression

As children progress between reading levels, observe how children cope with the increasing level of complexity in terms of both text and learning objectives. Additionally, you may need to evaluate and note the characteristics of individual children. Perhaps some children ask sensible questions about the text, while others rely too heavily on one reading strategy. Children are making good progress when able to read fluently and expressively, and respond to punctuation. Above all, they must show good understanding of the books they are reading, whether fiction or non-fiction, demonstrating this, for example, through their discussion and response. The Reading Response pages at the end of each *Collins Big Cat* book give you an immediate 'way in' to checking overall understanding, and to discussion.

Collins Big Cat assessment support

The Reading Response pages in every *Collins Big Cat* guided reading book offer an immediate assessment opportunity for teachers. Each one is designed to stimulate children's discussion and recapping of a text and this allows the teacher to check and assess children's comprehension of what they have just read.

During each guided reading session, a teacher using the photocopiable **Ongoing Record sheets** (pp135 to 137) can note each child's particular weaknesses and strengths, and then identify the necessary action needed to rectify weaknesses to build on strengths. For example, an improving and confident reader might be offered a

supported extension activity, such as internet research. A hesitant reader might require direct teaching of a reading skill, perhaps additional strategies for solving unfamiliar words. Children in either category might benefit from a move to a reading band more closely matched to their attainment level.

The **Ongoing Records** are linked to each *Collins Big Cat* book band, and provide generic band objectives. Teachers and assistants can check that children reading at any level are meeting band objectives while fulfilling the learning objectives specific to each book.

The **Reading Skills sheets** (pp138–140) provide a method of matching a child's attainment to a suitable book band, and can also be used to check children are reading at the correct level. The sheets should not be used for continuing assessment, but as a periodic check that a child has progressed in various key reading skills. The sheets can be used similarly to reading records, noting intervention or teaching action related to a child's difficulties in acquiring a specific reading skill.

Collins Big Cat's **Resources and Records Manager CD-ROM** provides a convenient, efficient and paper-free way to keep records for each child or group's progress and reading history. These can be used to inform the choice of intervention and help with selecting appropriate books to support individual children or groups.

In addition, **Half-Term Assessment Sheets** (p141) allow the teacher to summarise a child's progress over a longer period as well as monitor the progress of each group as a whole. These can be used in conjunction with **Half-Term Planning Notes** (p142).

Individual ongoing record (Lilac/Band 0)

Name _____ **Group** _____

At Lilac look to see if the reader:

- Identifies the parts of book – cover, title, page
- Opens the book and looks at pages in right order
- Understands the story/text and can talk about it

Date/book	Session objectives	Specific strengths and weaknesses	Next steps

Collins Big Cat Assessment and Support Guide A

Individual ongoing record (Pink/Band 1)

Name _____   Group _____

At Pink look to see if the reader:

- Opens the book, turns pages correctly and reads text left to right
- Matches spoken to written words
- Locates familiar words and uses pictures to check reading

Date/book	Session objectives	Specific strengths and weaknesses	Next steps

Collins Big Cat Assessment and Support Guide A

Individual ongoing record (Red/Band 2)

Name _____   Group _____

At Red look to see if the reader:

- Uses known words to check reading
- Reads with phrasing while tracking the text correctly
- Predict from meaning, syntax and print to solve new words

Date/book	Session objectives	Specific strengths and weaknesses	Next steps

Collins Big Cat Assessment and Support Guide A

Individual Reading Skills Sheet
(Lilac/Band 0)

Name _____   **Group** _____

Skill	Score*	Action
Sits and looks at a book for a time		
Finds the cover and turns the pages correctly		
Knows book terms *book, cover, title, page, word, beginning, end*		
Relates book to own experience		
Understands story structure – beginning, middle and end		
Predicts events in book, including ending		
Retells book in own words		

*Score key
1 = struggling
2 = progressing
3 = skill secured

Collins Big Cat Assessment and Support Guide A

Individual Reading Skills Sheet (Pink/Band 1)

Name _____   Group _____

Skill	Score*	Action
Locates title, opens book and turns pages in order		
Understands left page is read before right		
Understands that we read print left to right		
Matches spoken to written word (one-to-one matching)		
Reads some high frequency words		
Locates familiar words and uses them to check reading		
Predicts storyline and some vocabulary		
Uses picture cues to predict words		
Uses meaning of text along with language patterns		
Uses initial and final letter cues to predict words		
Understands elements of stories, character, sequence of events		
Understands how information can be found in non-fiction texts		
Retells narrative in sequence, drawing on language patterns		

Collins Big Cat Assessment and Support Guide A

*Score key
1 = struggling
2 = progressing
3 = skill secured

Individual Reading Skills Sheet (Red/Band 2)

Name _____   Group _____

Skill	Score*	Action
Is secure in one-to-one matching		
Uses known words to check reading		
Reads more rhythmically, using phrases		
Reads high frequency words		
Repeats words, phrases or sentences to check own reading		
Predicts new words from meaning		
Predicts new words from language pattern and print		
Reads words by blending letters		
Identifies capital letters and full stops		
Uses some storybook language when retelling story		
Describes main story settings, events and principal characters		
Reads with some expression		
Finds information in non-fiction text in response to where, who, how and why		

*Score key
1 = struggling
2 = progressing
3 = skill secured

Collins Big Cat Assessment and Support Guide A

Collins Big Cat

Half-termly Group Assessment Sheet

Class _____

Term _____

Group _____

Book band _____

Group objectives _____

_____

_____

Child's name	Books used and date	Reading	Responding to text	Evaluation and next steps

Review date _____

Next objectives _____

Collins Big Cat Assessment and Support Guide A

Half-termly Planning Notes

Class _____ Term _____ Group _____

Session sequence	Session 1	Session 2	Session 3	Session 4	Session 5	Session 6
Book title						
Getting started						
Reading and responding						
Returning to the book						
Checking and moving on						

My book review

Book title _____

Author _____

This book is: ☺ ☐   😐 ☐   ☹ ☐

It is about:

I liked:

I didn't like:

Reading band matching chart

Collins Big Cat*	IR band (Individualised Reading)**	Kaleidoscope Reading Sets***
Lilac Band 0	0 (red)	
Pink A Band 1A	1 (yellow)	
Pink B Band 1B	2 (white)	
Red A Band 2A	3 (dark blue)	YELLOW
Red B Band 2B	4 (pink)	
Yellow Band 3	5 (brown)	
Blue Band 4	6 (green)	
Green Band 5	7 (grey)	
Orange Band 6		RED
Turquoise Band 7	8 (orange)	
Purple Band 8		
Gold Band 9	9 (black)	
White Band 10		BLUE
Lime Band 11	10 (beige)	

* Similar to Reading Recovery National Network book bands
** National Centre for Language and Literacy
*** Books for Students